What People Are Saying…

As a recovering self-help-book reader, I was initially resistant to reading Pat's book. How could there be anything left to say on the subject of improving one's life?

Turns out there's plenty to say (and real-world practice to reinforce the ideas). This book isn't a read-through, isn't that interesting, put it down and go on to the next thing. It challenges you to *practice* what it teaches, and that makes all the difference.

~Christy Strauch, Author
CEO, Small Business Warrior

This is a great first step in beginning your journey of health and self-discovery.

~Dr. Jean-Luc LeProvost, Naturopathic Physician

I have been on my road to self discovery for years. *The Practical Guide to Figuring Yourself Out* workbook was an excellent tool that allowed me to finally piece together the parts of my life that I didn't even know had been holding me back, but, just as importantly, to notice those things that are strengths. The workbook provided me a starting point for how to move forward without my past continuing to creep up in unexpected ways and mess up my progress.

~Karen Merkley, B.A., Teacher

Journeys, good and bad, begin somewhere. Pat Honiotes in *The Practical Guide to Figuring Yourself Out and How to Go From Stuck to Star of Your Life* is a good place to start. The voice of Pat the Teacher is very prominent in this workbook. The heart of Pat as a healer is evident in each explanation, instruction, and encouragement. Pat provides a very clear explanation of how the workbook can be used, not once, but many times to keep growing going. It has been said *change is inevitable, but growth is an option*. If growth is your choice, the clear definitions, and the meaningful images used in this workbook will have great value.

Of the many good descriptions, I enjoyed the discussion about the many ways a person can die, physically, mentally, and spiritually resulting in a Walking Zombie Syndrome. Beyond being stuck at an earlier time of growth and awareness, as in the Ponce de Leon Syndrome, Pat provides insight and practical steps to reclaim a lost life due to the Walking Zombie Syndrome and getting unstuck due to the Ponce de Leon Syndrome. Journeys must begin somewhere. Pat's workbook is a good place to start when you are ready to *Figure Yourself Out* and *Go From Stuck to Star of Your Life*.

~Nicholas Cooper-Lewter, MSW, PHD, LISW-CP, Certified Personal and Executive Life Coach

This book was a gem. Concepts seemed to relate directly to me. Unlike other volumes in this genre, I was happily compelled to complete the exercises. I see this book as a road. The energy put forth in the exercises determines how far down that road you are willing to go. Keep the book handy! You will reference it again and again.

~Mike Fishburne, Real Estate

Pat writes with the voice of simplicity and directness enabling readers to focus on themselves instead of having to decipher the nature of the text. Her clarity and insights will help almost anyone on their journey.

~Dr. Kenneth Miller, Phoenix College

Ever heard the expression "you are your own worst enemy?" If you ever want that to change, then you need the right tools to help guide you to turn that enemy into a friend who helps you and gets out of your way as you reach for the life you've always wanted and always deserved. The way I figure it, Pat Honiotes has written a practical, hands-on workbook that really helps you to work out a lot of the blocks that stand between you and what your heart most desires. I'd recommend this to anyone who seriously wants to be their best self and reach for the stars.

~Chris Cayer, Competitive Intelligence Specialist, COO, Reyactive LLC.

THE PRACTICAL GUIDE TO
Figuring Yourself Out

How to Go from Stuck to Star of Your Life

Patricia J. Honiotes, M.S.

The opinions expressed in this manuscript are solely the opinions of the author and do not represent the opinions or thoughts of the publisher. The author has represented and warranted full ownership and/or legal right to publish all the materials in this book.

The Practical Guide to Figuring Yourself Out
How to Go From Stuck to Star of Your Life
All Rights Reserved.
Copyright © 2013 Patricia J. Honiotes, M.S.

www.PatHoniotes.com
www.FiguringYourselfOut.com

Cover Design by Tanja Tadic Imprint

Photos:
John Foley   www.tenthplaceproductions.com
Nancy Heimstra   www.NancyHeimstra.com
Lauren Potter   Lpotterphx@gmail.com

Designs:
Elisabeth Samuels   www.salterrasite.com

This book may not be reproduced, transmitted, or stored in whole or in part by any means, including graphic, electronic, or mechanical without the express written consent of the publisher except in the case of brief quotations embodied in critical articles and reviews.

Published by Healing Energies, Inc.
www.HealingEnergiesProcess.com

ISBN: 978-0-578-13047-7

PRINTED IN THE UNITED STATES OF AMERICA

Disclaimer

This book in no way takes the place of counseling, therapy or medical care. It is intended for educational purposes only. The information, exercises and techniques in this book are to be used at your own discretion. The author and publisher assume no responsibility or liability for your decision.

Contents

Acknowledgements		i
Ways to Use This Book		iii
Chapter 1	Introduction	1
Chapter 2	Step 1: Self-Assessment Forms	5
	Symptoms Worksheet	7
	Life Awareness Worksheet	9
	Words and Phrases Exercise	15
	Tree Exercise	17
Chapter 3	Step 2: Understanding the Basic Concepts	20
	Basic Concept 1:	
	Intellect vs. Experience	
	Thinking vs. Feeling	20
	Basic Concept 2:	
	Conscious vs. Subconscious	30
	Basic Concept 3:	
	Walking Zombie Syndrome	35
	Basic Concept 4:	
	Ponce de Leon Syndrome	39
	Basic Concept 5:	
	Your Primary Learning Mode	42
	Additional Resources for Chapter 3	45

Chapter 4	Step 3: Apply the Basic Concepts	47
	Bringing It All Together	47
	Symptoms Worksheet	49
	Life Awareness Worksheet	53
	Words and Phrases Exercise	65
	The Tree Exercise	70
	Summary Sheet	76
	Summary Sheet Exercise	78
	Additional Resources for Chapter 4	81
Chapter 5	Your Process and What to Expect	83
	The Way It Works	83
	The Coil Theory	89
	Elisabeth Kubler-Ross' *Five Stages of Grief*	93
	Additional Resource for Chapter 5	96
Chapter 6	Step 4: Understanding What Is Keeping You Stuck	97
Chapter 7	Steps to Take and Tools to Help You	108
Chapter 8	Clean and Clear Communication	114
	Being a Mature and Empowered Speaker	114
	Being a Mature and Empowered Listener	118
	Specific Guidelines for Clean and Clear Communication	121
	Non-verbal Communication	122
	Mixed Messages	123
Chapter 9	Setting and Honoring Boundaries	127
	Setting Boundaries vs. Manipulation	131
	Questions to Ask Yourself When Setting Boundaries	132
	Remember	135

Chapter 10	Goals, Affirmations and Achieving	137
	The Difference between Goals and Affirmations	137
	Why Use Goals?	138
	How Do Goals Really Work?	138
	Six Steps to Setting Powerful Goals	139
	Affirmations and How They Work	148
	Tips and Guidelines for Wording Your Affirmations	149
	When Affirmations Aren't "Working"	151
	Goals and Affirmations Worksheet	152
Bibliography		156
Appendix		157
	Duly Noted!!!	158
	Symptoms Worksheet	159
	Life Awareness Worksheet	161
	Words and Phrases Exercise	166
	Tree Exercise	168

Acknowledgements

I wish to take this opportunity to express my appreciation to all those who have contributed richly to not only the experiential content of this book but to my own personal life experience as well. Thank you to all my teachers and coaches who have taught me and guided me over the years.

A special thank you to the clients who "tested" the material in this book and let me know where I was unclear and gave me advice on how to fix it.

An extra special thank you goes to all the great editors who gave freely of their time to edit this book. I appreciate your work and the dedication you had for this project. Should the reader find any errors, they are due solely to last minute changes on my part.

Ways to Use This Book

There are three ways to use this book. One is to thumb through the book and read the parts that look interesting and maybe put one or two of them into action or, maybe put none of them into action. The problem with this approach is you are not going to learn much about yourself.

Another way to use this book is to read the book cover to cover and rarely, if ever, do any of the exercises. In either case, you might have a more intellectual understanding of yourself. Maybe. But, I'm pretty sure your life will not change much.

Another way to use this book is to read a chapter and do the exercises in that chapter before moving on to the next. Take your time with the exercises. Complete each exercise as honestly with as much detail as you can. This involves more than just filling in the blanks. Sometimes it may take days to fully complete the exercises. The biggest challenge of using the book this way is to remember to have patience and remember to practice what you are learning as you go along. In order to get the most benefit from this book you will need to put the time and energy into going through the steps and doing the exercises. Using the book this way is going to move you much closer to figuring yourself out and becoming the star of your life!

For those of you who are auditory learners, reading the book out loud may serve you. Sometimes reading something aloud can help you get more clarity about what the author is saying.

Take your time going through the exercises. The one who finishes the book first doesn't win anything. Give yourself and your mind time to digest what you are reading and practicing. Taking your time will likely keep you from feeling overwhelmed. There is a lot of information with a lot of experiencing in this book. While you may be a fast reader and a fast learner, this journey really cannot be hurried.

Keep something else in mind. This book is designed so you can reuse it again and again. All you have to do is update your new information and apply the concepts you learned the first time you completed the book. Actually, the understanding and clarity about a situation will come easily and more quickly each time because you will already have had some experience with the concepts.

Many times when we are trying to concentrate other thoughts come into our mind and distract us. I encourage you to have a DULY NOTED sheet handy so you can quickly jot down what has come into your mind. This way you can more easily regain focus on what you were reading. You may be surprised to find that while working in this book you have also come up with a grocery list, an errands list or a whole page of whining and complaining. What you put on the list is for your eyes only so write down briefly what you need to get off your mind so you can go back to concentrating on what you want to accomplish.

In the Appendix you will find a DULY NOTED sheet you can copy (for your private use only). The DULY NOTED sheet is useful when you are completing projects or activities and need to stay focused. If you'd rather, you may also go to the website to download a copy. www.FiguringYourselfOut.com. Click download forms and print the pdf form.

I know it's tempting to skip the introduction
BUT
please read it anyway.

Photo by Lauren Potter

CHAPTER 1
Introduction

The journey you are about to take is like putting together a puzzle. You are the puzzle. When you have all the pieces and they are in the proper place you have a clear, complete picture that makes sense. You also have all you need in order to live a more fulfilling life. Problems happen when you are missing pieces of the puzzle or you have put the pieces together incorrectly. In order for you to have the life you want, it is necessary for you to reclaim the pieces of your life you have lost.

Most people don't realize they have lost pieces of their life. If you are human, there are probably areas in your life in which pieces of you are missing. Having pieces of you missing can cause your life to be a great big mess! You can never complete the puzzle that is your life without those pieces. Depending upon what pieces are missing you may come close, but no matter how close you come you can never complete the puzzle until you find those missing pieces. The purpose of this book is to help you find the pieces of yourself you have lost and then show you how to reclaim those pieces and make sure you put them back in the right place.

This book will give you clear, basic explanations of concepts and theories that can sometimes be confusing. It is important for you to understand these concepts and theories in order to take the steps to figuring out what makes you tick, what may be holding you back in life and how to reclaim the pieces of your life.

This book is straightforward and sometimes blunt, with down-to-earth ideas and suggestions of actions you can take. It offers practical experiences that are focused and targeted. This book will give you the ground work to help you find, inside yourself, the information you need to:

- empower yourself in relationships
- gain prosperity
- set and honor your boundaries
- communicate more effectively
- increase your self expression
- improve your financial health
- reduce stress
- increase your self worth
- deal better with your work/career issues
- add fun and balance in your life

In short, this book gives you step-by-step learning and an action plan to guide you through the process to figuring yourself out and reclaiming your life.

In Step 1 you will fill in the self-assessment forms that will give you some clarity about where you are right now.

In Step 2 you will learn the *Basic Concepts* you need to know in order to interpret and understand the information you received in Step 1.

Step 3 will show you how to apply the concepts you learned in Step 2 to your own situation by using your personal information from the self-assessment forms.

Step 4 will help you identify what is blocking you and show you how to overcome those blocks.

During your journey through this book you are going to be asked to complete the exercises and experiences in each chapter. There will be basic intellectual information in each chapter that will give you what you need in order to participate in the activities and experiences of the chapter. Some people are going to be tempted to go straight to the study sheets and the action plans without first reading the chapter. Taking a short cut won't work! Thinking you already know won't work either! Be open to the information and the experiences in the chapters.

For those readers who want additional information on the concepts presented, suggestions for well-researched books and websites are provided at the end of some chapters.

There is one very important thing for you to keep in mind as you go through this book. And that is.....this journey is all about *you*. At this point anyone else's opinion or viewpoint just plain doesn't matter. Focus on you and what you think and feel. I am asking you to be self-centered on this journey. Make yourself the center of your world and be concerned with your own interests and needs. By doing this you are *not* being selfish. Selfish is taking something away from another person. You are not taking anything away from anyone else. You are giving to yourself. It is when your needs are being met that you can truly tend to the interests and needs of others, if necessary or appropriate. You've probably heard this before. However, remember when the airplane flight attendant gives the demonstration regarding the air masks, they always tell you to put your own oxygen mask on first before attempting to help someone else. The same idea applies here as well. You can't help someone else if you are not getting life-saving oxygen yourself.

The first step is for you to complete the *Symptoms Worksheet*, the *Life Awareness Worksheet*, the *Words and Phrases Exercise* and the *Tree Exercise* in Chapter 2. It is in your best interest to complete these exercises before reading any further in the book. The worksheets and the exercises are much more valuable and accurate if you fill them out before reading and understanding the thinking behind them. It enables you to give much more authentic, unbiased answers. You will bring all this information together in Chapter 4.

And, yes, it is possible for someone to manipulate the outcomes of the exercises. And, yes, there are those who will look ahead and figure out what they want the exercise to say. And, yes, you may get some answers you don't like or don't want to admit. Some of you may be tempted to change your answers to give yourself the impression your life is fine. If you are genuinely interested in taking this journey to figure yourself out, *why* would you do that?

Filling out the worksheets and doing the exercises in Chapter 2 is likely to "stir the bucket" and bring up some memories you haven't thought about in a very long time. Some of these things may make you uncomfortable. Maybe some of the things that come out will even make you mad or make you feel bad. Then you may wonder why in the world you would want to continue this journey. You would continue this journey because these exercises will begin to give you awareness. It is with this awareness you can make better choices and enjoy the personal freedom that is your birthright. This is not going to happen right after you finish Chapter 2. Remember, this is a journey and Chapter 2 is only the first step.

CHAPTER 2

Step 1: Self-Assessment Forms

One of the first steps to figuring yourself out is to recognize and understand where you are right now. That is the purpose of the worksheets in this chapter. It is really difficult to get to where you want to go when you don't know where you are starting.

Think about this example: if you want to take a road trip to visit your friend in Chicago and you live in Denver, you must recognize and admit you live in Denver. You may hate living in Denver with the snow and cold weather. So you imagine you live in Phoenix with the sunshine and warm weather. You so frequently imagine you live in Phoenix you really begin to believe you live in Phoenix.

There are some folks who so badly want to believe they are whatever it is they want to be but aren't, or want to believe they have no issues, that they ignore and deny the evidence and situations that tell them differently. They must admit who they are, warts and all, and where they are right now before they can truly be their potential. Just like no matter how much you really want to live in Phoenix, you cannot get to Chicago from Denver if you refuse to see you are really living in Denver. It is just as important to know and accept where you are starting your personal journey towards figuring yourself out.

The first worksheet to fill in is the *Symptoms Worksheet*. Please keep in mind there are no RIGHT answers; there are no WRONG answers; there are only YOUR answers.

If you prefer to download copies of the worksheets from the website, go to www.FiguringYourselfOut.com. Click *Download Forms* and print the pdf form.

Next fill in the *Life Awareness Worksheet*. Be as honest and complete as you possibly can. This information is for your eyes only and you share it only if *you* want to share it. Relax and take your time in filling it out. Complete this worksheet before you go on to the rest of the worksheets in this chapter. If you think of something more as you go through this book, you can always come back and fill it in later.

As you finish each worksheet immediately move on to the next one. You will be using all the worksheets from this chapter in Chapter 4 where you learn how to bring this information together in order to begin to figure yourself out. An important thing to remember while you are filling out the worksheets is to stop judging your answers and stop judging yourself. Have no opinions while you are completing these worksheets.

Remember, there are no RIGHT answers; there are no WRONG answers. There are only YOUR answers. Especially remember to drop any opinions or judgments you may have about your answers.

Symptoms Worksheet

So, how do you know if you have "checked out" or lost pieces of yourself? Mostly, your life will be out of balance. You will experience extremes of normal everyday "stuff" like sleeping too much or not being able to sleep at all. You may notice a big decrease in your appetite or a big increase in your appetite. You may experience no interest in sex or an extremely high interest in sex. Remember, the key here is *extremes*. Take some time now and complete the awareness worksheet below.

Please circle yes or no to each of the questions below. More often than not do you…

Say "yes" when you want to say "no?"	Yes	No
Say "I don't need any help," when you do?	Yes	No
Say "That doesn't bother me," but it does?	Yes	No
Say "Just one more drink won't hurt."	Yes	No
Say "I am not mad," when you really are?	Yes	No
Say "I can quit smoking any time I want."	Yes	No
Say "I am fine. Everything is okay," when it isn't?	Yes	No
Say "I can drop this weight any time I want," but you don't?	Yes	No
Smile when you really want to snap?	Yes	No
Bite your tongue when you have something to say.	Yes	No

Are you experiencing any of these on a regular basis?		
Feeling unreasonably tired	Yes	No
Loss of confidence	Yes	No
Procrastination	Yes	No
Inability to sleep	Yes	No
Sleeping too much	Yes	No
Eating binges	Yes	No
Feeling like a total failure	Yes	No
Lack of excitement for life	Yes	No
Spending binges	Yes	No
Guilt	Yes	No
Anxiety	Yes	No
Lack of joy	Yes	No

Life Awareness Worksheet

Name _____

Birthday _____

Birth Place _____

Time of birth _____

1. What's the problem (your primary concerns or issues)? Please use complete sentences.

   _____
   _____
   _____
   _____
   _____

2. How long has this been a problem for you?

   _____
   _____
   _____
   _____
   _____

3. Present Occupation: _____

   Like/dislike your job? _____

   If you could do anything you wanted as an occupation, what would it be?

   _____
   _____
   _____
   _____

4. Life Scale

On a scale of 0-10 (10 being the absolute best, 0 being the absolute worst)	
Looking at everything that is going on in your life, what number are you right now?	
What is the lowest number you have ever been in your whole life?	
What is the highest number you have ever been in your whole life?	

5. When you were born or when your mother was carrying you, was there any kind of a problem?

_____

_____

_____

_____

6. List all childhood diseases and, if possible, the age at which you had the disease.

_____

_____

_____

_____

7. List any hospitalizations or surgeries and the age you were when they occurred.

_____

_____

_____

_____

8. List any current medical conditions.

_____
_____
_____
_____

9. List any traumatic events in your life and the age at which they occurred. What is important to keep in mind here is whether it was traumatic for YOU.

_____
_____
_____
_____

10. Make a list of things in your life you feel guilty about and your age at the time the guilt started.

_____
_____
_____
_____

11. List what you consider to be your successes.

_____
_____
_____
_____
_____

12. Is there anything in your life you don't want anyone to find out about?

_____
_____
_____
_____
_____

13. Write down anything else you think might be helpful to you in achieving more awareness in your life. For example: income level, educational level, relationships, etc.

_____
_____
_____
_____
_____

You may want to take a break, even if it is a short one, before going on to the *Words and Phrases Exercise.*

The *Words and Phrases Exercise* is intended to be completed in one sitting and in less than five minutes. You may be tempted to *think* about your response rather than just writing down the first thing that comes into your mind. *Please avoid that temptation.*

Start with Number 1 and respond to each word or phrase in order. **Do not** skip it and "come back later." Respond quickly, without thought or explanation. If you "draw a blank" on one of the words or phrases, that's okay, skip it and move on.

The most effective and easiest way to respond to this exercise is to go to www.FiguringYourselfOut.com. Click *Audio Exercise.* Click *"Listen"* and respond as I read the words and phrases to you. The audio will help you answer quickly and with as little thought as possible. Listen to the audio only once.

Relax as much as possible while completing the *Words and Phrases Exercise.* Remember, there are no RIGHT answers. There are no WRONG answers. There are only YOUR answers. Especially remember to drop any opinions or judgments you may have about your answers.

Words and Phrases Exercise

Listed below are a number of various words, thoughts and phrases. Please respond quickly with the very first word, thought, phrase, emotion or idea that pops into your mind.

1. Sweet	
2. Fear	
3. Anger	
4. If only	
5. There must be	
6. I know I'm stressed when I	
7. I always	
8. All my life	
9. I felt like dying when	
10. Red	
11. I'm just like	
12. Please	
13. It all started when	
14. Kindness	
15. Death	

16. I don't want to disappoint	
17. I'm just tired of	
18. It got worse when	
19. I never	
20. Success	
21. Exercises like this	
22. Begin a sentence with the word, "who"	
23. Career	
24. Confidence	
25. Relax	

As before, it may serve you to take a break before going on to the *Tree Exercise*. Take your time drawing your tree.

STOP judging your artistic ability and have fun with this one.

Tree Exercise

In the space provided below, draw a tree.

1. Draw a line across the top of the tree, like the top of the tree has hit the ceiling.
2. Draw a line at the base of the tree (where it meets the ground).
3. Draw another line midway between the top line and the bottom line.
4. Draw another line halfway between the middle line and the top line.
5. Draw another line halfway between the middle line and the bottom line. Your tree should now be divided into 4 equal parts.
6. Write your present age on the top line.
7. Put a zero on the bottom line.
8. Divide your present age by 2. Put that number on the middle line.
9. Divide the number on the middle line by 2. Put that number on the line between the middle line and the bottom line.
10. Take the number that is on the line between the middle and the bottom line and add it to the number on the middle line. Put this new number on the line between the middle line and the top line.

You may find it challenging to put aside your curiosity about what your answers *mean* on your self-assessment forms. While it may be tempting to skip Chapter 3 and move on to Chapter 4 to get it all figured out, please resist the temptation! The information you learn in Chapter 3 is crucial in helping you understand the work in Chapter 4.

It may also be challenging for you to let go of your opinions and judgments about your responses on the worksheets in this current chapter. If you go through this chapter, or any other, upset because you are the way you are or judging it is unfair or really bad you have the symptoms and history you have, you will stay stuck right where you are. Do the best you can to drop your opinions and judgments about your responses and begin to be more accepting of yourself and where you are beginning your journey. When you can do that, it will make understanding the concepts in Chapter 3 much easier.

Hint: You can write down your judgments on the DULY NOTED sheet. If they come up again, write them down again. If they come up again, write them down again. Write them down as many times as they come up for you.

"The greatest obstacle to your health and well being is the subconscious disconnection from your emotions."
~Dr. Darren Weissman~

CHAPTER 3

Step 2: Understanding the Basic Concepts

Basic Concept 1:
Intellect vs. Experience
Thinking vs. Feeling

In the past, I have occasionally been accused of dismissing the intellect or saying the intellect is not important. Nothing could be further from the truth. We absolutely need our intellect to survive. We need our intellect to help us solve problems and think critically. The trouble starts when we make our brain king and ignore our feelings and experiences. This causes a problem I refer to as helmet understanding. Helmet understanding means you get it from your neck up; you get it in your brain. You understand it. You can probably even explain it. However, it doesn't mean you have integrated the concept and are able to use it in your everyday life.

When explaining helmet understanding to clients, I am often reminded of a friend who wanted to play the piano. She took piano lessons weekly for a very long time. She knew all about the proper posture and finger placement. She knew all about time signatures. She learned all the keys on the piano and memorized the scales. In fact, she was so good she could even teach others how to play the piano. She could show them the correct hand positions. She could explain scales to them and teach them the value of each note. However, she couldn't play a single song on the piano! This was because all she had was the helmet (brain) understanding of how to play the piano. She had taken little or no time to practice the piano and learn from the experience. Maybe she didn't like the feeling associated with practicing the piano. Maybe she didn't like the feeling of not playing well enough. It is pretty obvious when learning to play the piano, practicing the piano is absolutely necessary. Her butt needed to be on the bench with her fingers on the keyboard in order for her to learn to play the piano!

Photo by John Foley

The same idea is true in all areas of life. If you are learning how to mow the lawn, cook dinner or fold the laundry, if you are learning to be in relationship, communicate better or write a book, if you are learning to be a doctor, lawyer or candle stick maker your butt needs to be on the bench with your fingers on the keyboard. You must practice, practice, practice and then practice some more. Just reading a book about any of those things or watching someone else practice cannot replace you practicing and you learning from the experience.

Why is it so hard for people to put their butts on the bench? Usually it is because they don't like how it *feels*. We have been taught not to feel. In many cases, we have been taught not to feel from the time we are born or even before. We have been taught to especially not feel uncomfortable feelings. We have been taught to avoid feelings and to definitely not express them under any circumstances. Not only that, we have been taught we shouldn't have to feel anything uncomfortable. Notice how quickly people in general take medicine for pain? Then there is the practice of taking the pain killer so it doesn't even start to hurt. So it is with feelings and experiences as well. We don't want to feel or experience anything that is not comfortable.

We have received messages throughout our whole lives that tell us not to feel, and if we do feel, whatever you do, don't *express* the feeling. Do any of these sentences sound familiar?

Salterra Design

The list could go on and on and on and on and on. In those simple statements the message is sent loud and clear…"don't feel, don't admit it if you do" and "don't express." Keep in mind you didn't necessarily get this message just through words. Some parents and teachers are masters of "the look."

Take a few minutes now to make a list of all the messages you remember receiving that said don't feel, don't admit it if you do and don't express a feeling. When you can remember, write down who gave you this message. Make this list as complete as possible and know you can always add to it as you go along.

_____
_____
_____
_____
_____
_____
_____
_____

Expressing feelings can make many people feel uncomfortable because it means they must first be in touch with themselves, and that, in and of itself, can make a lot of people uncomfortable. Others around them expressing their feelings can make them feel just as uncomfortable. Feeling uncomfortable is when people may respond with some of the above statements. Usually those who make statements like the ones above have lost contact with themselves and, as a result, have ignored, denied and not expressed their own feelings. They haven't given themselves permission to connect, to feel and to express. If they don't have permission for themselves, it is impossible for them to give it to someone else. As a result, the pattern of shut-down feelings is passed on from generation to generation.

Without the permission to feel and express we are left with the intellect. Again, the intellect is not less than experience. It is an important and necessary partner. Remember, in order to have complete learning intellect and experience must be in balance.

It is as an adult you need to give yourself permission to connect, to experience and express. What a gratifying feeling it is to connect and open yourself to a *complete* experience of you!

Keep in mind a door cannot be open and closed at the same time. Neither can your mind. If you are not staying in touch with yourself, are closed to experiencing emotions that are not much fun, you are also closed to experiencing full joy and other fun emotions.

An exercise that is very useful in becoming more aware of you and your feelings is the *Stay in Touch* exercise. Look at it this way. Whether you have just met a new person or want to continue a friendship with someone you already know, keeping in touch with that person on a regular basis is critical to a healthy, enduring relationship. The same thing is true for your relationship with you. In order to have a healthy and enduring relationship with yourself you must stay in touch with yourself.

Think about the ways you keep in touch with people you care about (email, text, phone, etc.). Use these same tools to keep in touch with yourself. Send yourself an email or text. Call and leave a voice message for yourself. Remember to check for these messages later in the day or evening.

So, your question may be, "What do I say in these messages to myself?"

Think about what you say in your messages to others that you care about. Maybe some of these would work for you:

- Love you
- Remember to …..
- Hope you have a great day
- Looking forward to ….. with you

On the lines below, write messages you would like to receive from yourself.

_____
_____
_____
_____
_____

When you receive the messages, stop for a second or three and get in touch with what you are feeling or experiencing. How did getting the message from yourself make you feel?

_____
_____
_____
_____
_____

You may want to write down the feeling or experience, or not. Be aware of how comfortable you are with whether or not you are able to connect with your feelings. The whole idea behind this exercise is to remind you to stay in touch with you and bring you into awareness about your feelings. Be aware of how comfortable you are with what you are feeling. In this exercise there is nothing for you to **do** with the feeling except experience it. I would suggest you do this exercise for thirty days. If you really want to learn to stay in touch with yourself and your feelings, do this exercise for three months or more. By the end of the three months you will have developed the beginning of a new pattern of paying attention to you and your feelings. You will probably know yourself a whole lot better too.

Take a few moments now to write down how you feel about doing the *Stay in Touch* exercise.

_____

_____

_____

_____

On the lines below, record what you learned about yourself by doing the *Stay in Touch* exercise.

_____

_____

_____

_____

By the way, good, fine and okay are not feelings. They are an evaluation of the feeling you are having. Whenever you find yourself feeling good, fine or okay ask yourself, "What feeling am I having that I believe is a good (or fine or okay) feeling?" When you can shift from the evaluation of the feeling and get to the feeling itself, it will help you become more connected with yourself.

Check what you wrote for the exercise above. If you felt good, fine or okay about doing the *Stay in Touch* exercise, take a few moments to write down what the feeling was you evaluated as being good, fine or okay.

_____

_____

_____

_____

When you have been in a pattern of shut-down around your feelings, it is sometimes difficult to connect with a feeling or know exactly what the feeling is. As a result, you may try to *think* a feeling. As soon as you try to think a feeling or figure out what the feeling is, it becomes a thought, not a feeling.

"This exercise is stupid," is a thought. "I feel stupid sending myself messages," is a feeling. "People are going to think I'm crazy," is a thought. "I feel self-conscious doing this exercise," is a feeling. Now go back and check. Did you express feelings or thoughts about doing the *Stay in Touch* exercise? If you expressed thoughts, take a few moments to write how you *feel* about doing the exercise.

_____

_____

_____

_____

_____

Keep in mind when you ask yourself how you are feeling and your answer is something like, "This is a waste of time," that is a thought. Try to get to the feeling underneath the thought. For example, what is the feeling you are having that makes you think the exercise is a waste of time? Even better, what feeling are you having that has you think the exercise might be fun and useful?

For the heck of it, take ten seconds right now to write down what you are feeling in this moment. Writing down the first thing that comes into your mind will help.

_____

_____

_____

_____

_____

Now check the exercise above. Did you write down feelings or thoughts? _____ If you wrote down a thought, go back and see what the feeling was.

A great idea … take another ten seconds right now to either text, email or leave a voice message for yourself.

One last thought about the intellect. The intellect can be a double-edged sword. It comes in handy when you are trying to figure out a math problem or the best route to the grocery store or figuring out the E major scale on the piano. Problems happen when you use your intellect as a defense.

When you use your brain to defend why you haven't been able to accomplish something or when you use it to defend being a real jerk to someone, that's a problem. Some people are able to convince themselves something is true (their route to the grocery store is best) even when they have been given evidence which clearly shows another route has less traffic and is fifteen miles shorter. Some people have the intellectual ability to justify anything. It is important for you to know when you are justifying and when you are being real. If you are fighting to be right, you are probably justifying. If you have a whole bunch of really good reasons and you are speaking them really fast, you are probably trying to convince yourself. So, stop and see what you are avoiding or denying.

While the intellect can be a double-edged sword, totally relying on feelings is a "butt-kicker" as well. Sometimes, some people rely so much on their feelings, without regard to their intellect they believe whatever they feel is true. They make their feeling mean something without checking it out to see if the feeling is accurate in a particular situation. For example, you may feel rejected or not important because a friend forgot to send you a birthday card. Yes, the possibility does exist your friend no longer wants anything to do with you and doesn't have what it takes to tell you. However, the possibility also exists the card was lost in the mail. Maybe your friend had a crisis or was overwhelmed and forgetting to send you a birthday card had absolutely nothing to do with you. This is not intended to make excuses for your friend. It is about checking out the facts before jumping to conclusions and running with it.

Remember, experience is not better than intellect and intellect is not better than experience. You need the balance of both to gain the most on your path to figuring yourself out.

So what does this have to do with figuring yourself out? When you understand you need both your intellect and your experience to have complete learning, it will make figuring yourself out a whole lot easier.

Basic Concept 2: Conscious vs. Subconscious

There have been hundreds of books written about the conscious and the subconscious mind. There is a huge amount of research on the subconscious mind and how it works. That is all very interesting and fascinating and at the end of this chapter there are several very good resources for those of you who wish to go into more depth on the subject.

For our purposes here we are going to use a very simple way to describe the difference between the conscious and the subconscious part of your mind. You are aware of the information in the conscious part of your mind. You are not aware of the information in the subconscious part of your mind. If you are given a math problem, you use your conscious mind to find the answer. Anytime you have to figure out an answer you are using the conscious part of your mind. Here is another example. Look at yourself and describe what you are wearing. Your description is coming from the conscious part of your mind. What may be subconscious is the reason *why* you are wearing what you are wearing. It may simply be it was the only clean outfit you had. Or, you may be wearing what you are wearing because of something stored in your subconscious mind, such as being made fun of for wearing colorful outfits so now you stick to very neutral colors. You may not even consciously remember the specific incident, but you are still reacting to it. The subconscious mind is where you store everything that has ever happened to you. When you are trying to gain a more complete understanding of yourself, what is in your subconscious mind can matter a great deal.

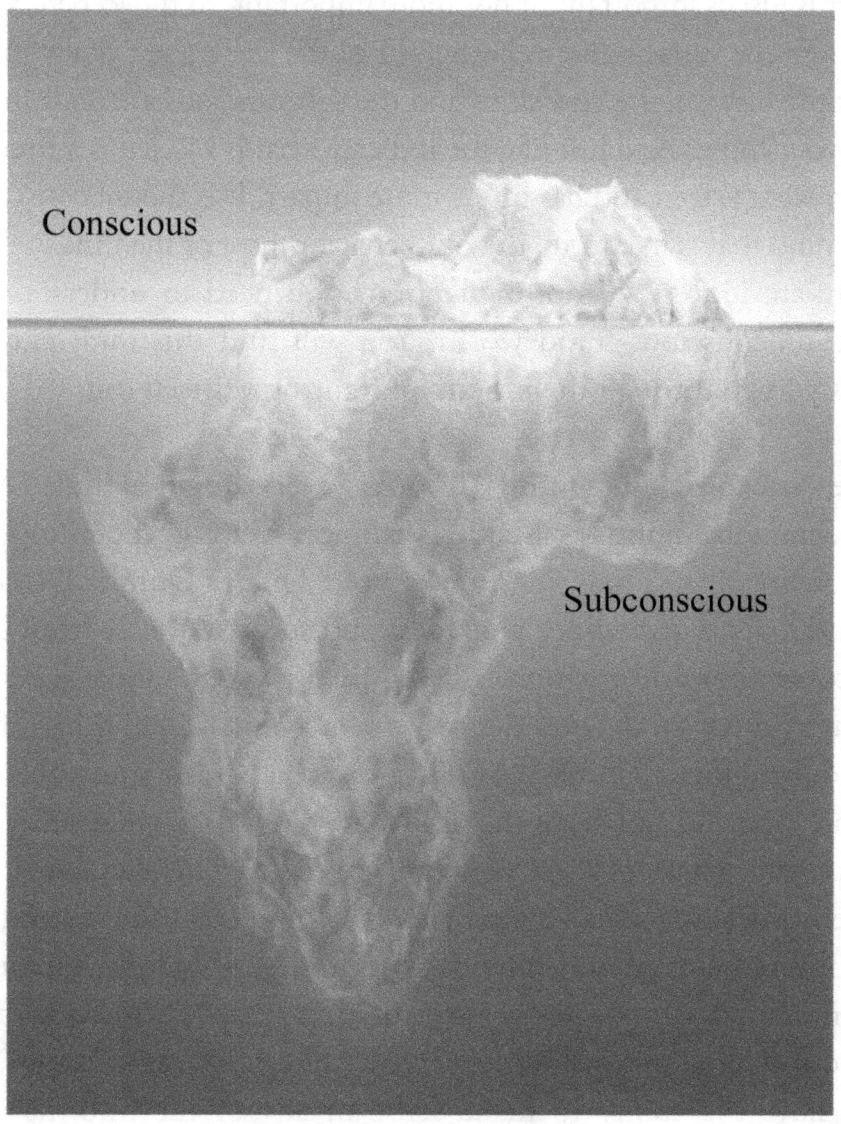

Salterra Design

Your conscious mind and your subconscious mind are very much like an iceberg. What you see above the water (conscious mind) is only a small part of what is below the surface (subconscious mind). What is hidden beneath the water is just as important, if not more important, to the iceberg as is what shows above the surface. Just as both parts of the iceberg are vitally important to the entire iceberg, the conscious and the subconscious are both important parts of your mind. And just like the iceberg, what is hidden is a much larger part than what is seen and has much more impact. It is the subconscious part of your mind that is in control of your behavior most of the time.

There are four very important points you need to understand about how the subconscious mind works. You will find this information very useful as you go through the process of figuring yourself out.

1. **The subconscious mind records everything.** Think of your subconscious mind as a filing cabinet. Within the filing cabinet are many files. These files are labeled Smart, Dumb, Dead, Alive, Confident, Worthwhile, Worthless and so on. At least from the time of conception information is being filed in your subconscious mind. That means even the experiences you had while still in the womb, such as your mother's emotions or illnesses, are a part of your subconscious mind. You did not have the ability to determine what emotion was yours and what emotion was your mother's. This can sometimes be where a person's issue begins. Your subconscious mind records all the emotional, mental and physical *stuff* going on before you were even born. Your birth process is also stored in your subconscious mind as is your experience inside the womb before you were born. You did not have the ability to make sense of any of the information, but the information is still there. Even as adults, the subconscious mind continues to record everything and we are not even aware of it most of

the time. Anything you have ever been exposed to has been recorded in the subconscious part of your mind.

2. **The subconscious mind is literal.** The subconscious mind records everything exactly as it receives it. It hears and records a situation *exactly* as it happened, without interpretation. The subconscious mind doesn't understand sarcasm or kidding. It is literal. Your subconscious mind takes what you have said and heard and records that information exactly. Examples: "I am so stupid." "I look ugly in this outfit." "I am just dead on my feet." What goes into the files in your subconscious mind are the words stupid, ugly and dead. So much for "sticks and stones can break my bones but words can never hurt me."

In much the same way, your subconscious mind does not hear contractions like don't or won't. It does pick up on the action word following the contraction. For example, "don't run," your mind hears "run." "I won't be nervous," your mind hears "nervous."

3. **The subconscious mind does not discern.** It stores the information exactly as it is received. It does not judge whether the information is right or wrong, accurate or inaccurate, good or bad. The subconscious mind does not understand "just kidding" or sarcasm. It merely files what is said or heard whether it is true or not. Remember, what is put into your subconscious mind comes out in your thoughts and actions without you even realizing it.

4. **The information in the subconscious mind is recallable given the right motivation and techniques.** Sometimes the information just comes out spontaneously. For example, you may be talking about your child's fifth

birthday and the party you are planning for them and, what seems like all of a sudden, the memory of your fifth birthday pops into your mind. A particular smell may cause a forgotten memory to suddenly come to mind. A scene in a movie or a stranger sitting in the restaurant can cause information to emerge from the subconscious mind. Almost anything can trigger a subconscious memory and bring it into your conscious mind. In figuring yourself out, you will want to trigger some memories on purpose which was part of the reason for the self-awareness worksheets and exercises.

So what does all this subconscious stuff have to do with figuring yourself out? Knowing there are things affecting your behavior you may not be aware of will give you the opportunity to look for what may be hidden from you that can be influencing your life. Now you can look for these things since you know they exist.

Knowing how the subconscious mind works also gives you the opportunity to update the information stored in your subconscious mind. You can never rid yourself of the information in the old files, but you can update your files to make them more accurate.

When you are working to figure yourself out, it is important for you to understand the subconscious mind and how it works. On the lines below write down the four qualities of the subconscious mind you need to stay aware of in order to figure yourself out. Then mark this page so it is easy to find when you are working on bringing your awareness exercises together in the next chapter.

_____

_____

_____

Basic Concept 3:
Walking Zombie Syndrome

Most of you have probably seen the old horror movies on late night TV. The zombie movies are the ones where the bodies of dead people move and act like they are really alive. The zombies are kind of wooden and listless and even though they move we know they are really dead inside. Zombie is what life can be like for those who are missing pieces of themselves. They may feel empty at times or may feel like something is missing. They go through the motions each day, but aren't fully alive according to their subconscious mind. There are many different degrees of the Walking Zombie Syndrome depending upon what the person has experienced and how much of themselves they have lost.

In order to completely understand the Walking Zombie Syndrome it is important to be aware there are at least three ways you can die. You can die physically. You can die emotionally. You can die spiritually. Because the subconscious mind is literal and doesn't know the difference between the different kinds of death or the difference between a death suggestion and actual death, all death suggestions are put in the dead file in the subconscious mind. This file can become so large the subconscious mind begins to accept "death" and the person may begin to act like the walking zombies we see in the movies.

1. **Physical Death and Death Suggestions.** A person may die physically, but then it's all over with and it doesn't really matter anyway. However, you can receive physical death suggestions where you didn't die physically, but your subconscious mind accepts death. A great example of this is surgery. Think about it. What do they do to you before they begin the surgery? They put you to "sleep." This kind of sleep is as close

to dying as you can get without really dying. You cannot speak. You cannot move. You have no control. They even breathe for you. Because your subconscious mind is literal and does not discern (dead people don't speak or move or breathe) surgery is a death suggestion in your subconscious mind.

Other examples of physical death suggestions:
- Diagnosis from a doctor you are going to die
- Severe enough injuries you thought you might die
- Accidents where you thought you might not make it
- Severe pain

2. **Emotional Death.** You let pieces of you die emotionally all the time. It's not a physical death suggestion but remember the subconscious mind does not know the difference between the different kinds of death. Death of any kind is just death and gets filed in the death file in the subconscious mind.

Examples of emotional death:
- Death of someone close to you
- Breakup of a relationship
- Embarrassing moments
- Graduation
- Losing a job
- Divorce
- Marriage
- Abortion (This affects the male as well as the female.)

Are you surprised marriage and graduation are included in the list of examples of emotional death? It is important to keep in mind the subconscious mind is literal. When someone marries, it is the death of their single life. It is also the beginning of a new married life. But it is still a death. Graduation is the beginning of a new professional life and it is also the death of school life.

What events have you had in your life that are both a death suggestion and a new, alive beginning?

_____

_____

_____

_____

_____

3. **Spiritual Death…The Death of the Soul.** Guilt is always spiritual death. Why? Because a great number of people have been taught if they do enough things wrong in their life they will go to hell. That would be the ultimate death of their soul. Guilt can also cause the death of self-worth and self-confidence. Any situation in which you receive a death suggestion can, and most often does, involve more than one category of death.

4. **Other Death.** Basically any death suggestion that does not fit into the other categories or a combination of several or all of the above categories is included in this category. Loss of money and loss of integrity are both examples of other death suggestions. Does this remind you of any other death suggestions in your life? If so, write them on the lines below.

_____

_____

_____

_____

_____

Bottom line is, it doesn't really matter in what category we put a death suggestion. The categories are only used to teach the concept. The idea here is to understand we receive death suggestions and they do influence us.

So what does the Walking Zombie Syndrome have to do with figuring yourself out? When you can understand you have lost pieces of yourself and this is preventing you from living the life you want, you can go about finding and reclaiming the pieces you've lost. The awareness you have lost pieces of yourself is golden. It is very rare for people to look for something they don't realize they've lost! Knowing you have lost pieces of yourself, you can now begin to look for and reclaim them.

You have learned about the Walking Zombie Syndrome. Take that knowledge and go back through your *Personal Life Awareness Worksheet* and add any other death suggestion situation you might have forgotten. Remember to add the age at which the incident happened, if possible.

Basic Concept 4:
Ponce de Leon Syndrome

Juan Ponce de Leon was a Spanish explorer who led the first European expedition to Florida. Legend has it Ponce de Leon discovered Florida while looking for the Fountain of Youth. Ponce de Leon believed if he drank the water from the Fountain of Youth he would be young forever. The Ponce de Leon Syndrome (PDL) is a term used to describe someone who has not emotionally matured in some areas of their life. It is as if they drank from the Fountain of Youth. Emotionally there are parts of them that are stuck at a much younger age. Their emotions have not matured at the same rate as their body. The problem with this is they, especially under stress, will respond and react from the mindset of a much younger age. Having a young child running your life, your business or your relationship doesn't usually work very well!

Have you ever seen an adult yelling at a server or clerk? This is an example of an adult stuck at a much younger age, at least in that particular moment. This is an example of an adult temper tantrum. Have you ever experienced an adult demanding they be served RIGHT NOW? Have you ever observed an adult kicking the soda machine, hitting the wall with their fist, crying if they don't get their way, refusing to speak or smoking in a no-smoking zone? What about the fifty year old woman who still wears mini-skirts and pigtails? What about the adult who spends all their money as soon as they get their paycheck? All these are examples of PDL behavior. An important part of this journey for you will be noticing where you have some PDL behaviors and how often you display the behaviors.

It would serve you to become familiar with the development of human beings. Having a general understanding of what is *normal* at different ages will help you pinpoint at what age you may be operating when you are in certain situations or under stress. When you can determine an approximate age, you can then go back and try to figure out if there was a traumatic or important event in your life at that time, which may have you emotionally stuck at that age. Then it's about healing so you can grow and mature beyond the younger age.

Examples of PDL behavior:
- Sense of entitlement (the world owes me syndrome)
- Thinking the world revolves around you
- Wanting it (whatever "it" is) and wanting it right now
- Temper tantrums when you don't get what you want
- Looking for love in unhealthy places and in unhealthy ways
- Being selfish
- Thinking you are the exception to the Laws of the Universe
- Crying when you don't get your way
- Throwing things or punching walls when you are angry
- Giving someone the silent treatment
- Gossiping
- Needing to be reassured excessively that you are loved, etc.
- Driving drunk
- Needing to be the center of attention
- Interrupting

There are also people who have reverse PDL Syndrome. They have had the child part of them held down for so long it is almost impossible for them to let go and have fun. They have a tendency to take themselves very seriously. For some, they were never allowed to be a child. They may have had to take on adult issues at a very early age or they may not have had permission to be a child and do child-like things. Whatever the reason, they were forced into adulthood, probably with adult responsibilities, at a very early age. They grow up resenting not having had a healthy childhood, resenting those who did have a healthy childhood and beat themselves up when they accidentally have a childish or child-like moment. Their ability to have fun, even adult fun, is very low. The missing part of their development needs to be brought back in order for them to lead a fulfilling life. In some cases, they may even have to learn how to have fun.

Take some time now to look and see where your behavior is sometimes, or a lot of the time, immature. Write down what your particular behaviors are during those times. You might also want to get feedback from someone you trust to see if you are missing something.

_____

_____

_____

_____

_____

If you perceive yourself as more of the reverse PDL, take some time now and write down the areas where you may take things, and yourself, way too seriously. Identify areas where you need to learn to have more fun.

_____

_____

_____

_____

_____

So what does the Ponce de Leon Syndrome have to do with figuring yourself out? When you begin to understand you are sometimes operating from a childish frame of mind, you can begin to see why some things in your life are not working. Simply being aware of these behaviors can give you more choice about your behavior. Knowing you have the PDL syndrome, you can begin to look and see what may have happened to you at a particular age, or didn't happen to you, that has kept you stuck there. You may never discover exactly what it was. That's okay. Frustrating? Maybe. But it's okay because you still have the insight telling you here is a place for you to look and see where you might have a part of you that needs to heal and grow.

Basic Concept 5:
Your Primary Learning Mode

There are primarily three ways in which people learn: auditory, visual and kinesthetic. Auditory is learning through hearing such as listening to CDs or tapes or a lecture. Visual learning is done through reading a book or watching a demonstration. Kinesthetic learning is done through feeling/touch and hands-on experience. One learning mode is not better than another. It is just a matter of knowing which mode your brain naturally likes the best so you can use that mode on purpose.

Everyone has a primary or natural way to learn. It is important for you to know your natural way to learn so you can make sure you use that way deliberately. Using your primary learning mode ensures you are giving yourself the best opportunity to learn. It doesn't mean you don't use the other ways to learn. Of course you do! Just make sure you are always using your natural way to learn.

Determine your primary learning mode. Pretend for a moment you are taking a test tomorrow morning on your ability to put a bicycle together. You will be given a box of bicycle parts and you will have two hours to put the bicycle together. You have this evening to prepare for the test. You may choose **one** of the following to learn how to put the bicycle together. Yes, only one!

    A. Look at a picture of the bicycle and maybe read the directions.
    B. Have someone tell you how to put the bicycle together.
    C. Have a box of bicycle parts and figure it out.

If you chose A, your primary way of learning is probably visual. If you chose B, your primary way of learning is most likely auditory. If you chose C, kinesthetic is probably your primary way of learning.

Based on this exercise, what do you think your **primary** learning mode is? Yes, choose only one.

_____

While this is a very simple, not very in-depth, or scientific way to determine your favorite way to learn, it will give you a start. Seriously consider using the resource book *Learn More Now* to help you determine your primary mode of learning. More information is available about this book at the end of this chapter.

What does knowing your primary way to learn have to do with figuring yourself out? When you know how you learn best, you can then make sure you put yourself in the best possible position and have the best tools for you to learn and to figure yourself out.

This is another chapter, like Chapter 2, where it may be challenging for you to let go of your opinions and judgments about yourself. If you go through this chapter upset because you are a Walking Zombie or have Ponce de Leon behaviors, you will stay stuck.

Remember from the Introduction the importance of knowing your starting place? Realizing you have lost pieces of yourself and you have some childish behaviors is your starting place. Remember, you must know where you are starting from in order to get where you want to go. You cannot reclaim pieces you don't realize you are missing and you cannot change a behavior if you don't realize you have the behavior to begin with. Relax and drop your opinion about where you are beginning your journey and let's move on to Chapter 4.

Additional Resources for Chapter 3

- If you want to learn more about the subconscious mind and how it works, *The Power of Your Subconscious Mind* by Joseph Murphy, Ph.D., D.D is an excellent resource. Murphy explains the subconscious mind in depth and he also gives you practical guidelines on how to make your subconscious mind work for you.
- *Learn More Now* by Marcia L. Conner is a fabulous book to help you determine your primary mode of learning. She also helps you determine your motivation for learning and your best atmosphere for learning. She gives you steps to follow to be able to learn better and faster. This book is filled with loads of exercises and tips.
- A great resource to understand how feelings impact your body is *The Inside Story: Understanding the Power of Feelings* available from HeartMath, LLC. The exercises they teach are very good. Keep in mind, even if you use those exercises, you still need to continue your journey to understanding yourself better and figuring yourself out.
- *The Secret Life of the UNBORN CHILD* by Thomas Verney, M.D. was written to guide parents in the care of their unborn child. Dr. Verney based the concepts in his book on over 20 years of medical research. Reading this book will give you amazing insights into your own prenatal and birth experiences.
- The information about the four attributes of the subconscious mind, the Walking Zombie Syndrome and the Ponce de Leon Syndrome is my interpretation of these topics that were presented at the professional courses I attended through the American Academy of Medical Hypnoanalysts and my training in the Academy's Clinical Training Program. If you would like more information on these concepts, contact the American Academy of Medical Hypnoanalysts or go to

their website, www.aamh.com, and order the following articles from their store:
- *The Walking Zombie Syndrome* by William J. Bryan, Jr., M.D.
- *Ponce de Leon Syndrome* by William J. Bryan, Jr., M.D.

CHAPTER 4

Step 3: Apply the Basic Concepts

Bringing It All Together

This chapter is called *Bringing It All Together* for a reason. Using what you have learned about the basic concepts in the last chapter, you will be able to put together, in a meaningful way, the valuable information you gathered about yourself on the Self-Assessment forms in Chapter 2. You will be able to see where you have lost pieces of yourself, see patterns and habits you have developed and where you learned your judgments, opinions, beliefs, expectations and rules.

By the end of your work in this chapter, you will have a pretty clear outline of where your issues started, what made them worse and why they continue to remain issues today. You can then use this outline to guide yourself in taking steps to begin healing, growing and reclaiming your life.

For the work in this chapter, you will need a copy of the *Summary Sheet* on page 78. If you wish, you can download a *Summary Sheet* from the website, www.FiguringYourselfOut.com. Click download forms and print the pdf form. You will also need the *Self-Assessment* forms you completed in Chapter 2. Keep all these forms handy as you will be using them constantly throughout this chapter.

At first glance, this chapter may seem overwhelming. Juggling the forms and the information and putting it in the appropriate place on the *Summary Sheet* may seem confusing. However, take the following steps and the process will be smooth and rewarding for you:

1. Take your time. Take breaks frequently. You don't have to finish it all in one day.
2. Follow the step-by-step instructions carefully and in order. Skipping around will only confuse and frustrate you.
3. It will be easier for you if you make a copy of your *Self-Assessment* forms and the *Summary Sheet*. That way you won't have to flip back and forth between the pages in this book. Put the worksheets to your side and keep them handy as you work through this chapter.
4. Use a pencil, with an eraser, when you are filling out the *Summary Sheet*. As you go through your information, it is very likely you will need to move some of the information around on your *Summary Sheet*.
5. If at any time you start feeling confused, stop. Re-read the *exact words* of the instructions and then proceed. Do not try to read anything into the instructions. Just follow the instructions *exactly*.
6. *Most important!* If you have not completed all the Self-Assessment forms in Chapter 2, do so before even thinking about beginning the process of bringing it all together. Make sure you have put as much detail into your responses as you possibly can. Having complete and detailed information on your forms will insure a much more accurate *Summary Sheet* and therefore, a more useful one. Take some time now and double check your worksheets and make sure they are complete. When they are as complete as you can make them, take out your *Symptoms Worksheet* and your *Summary Sheet* and let's get started.

Symptoms Worksheet

The *Symptoms Worksheet* is an awareness exercise. It helps you become aware of symptoms you didn't know you had or maybe you didn't realize they were symptoms. First of all, how many of these symptoms did you circle "yes?"_____

The truth is there is nothing magical about how many items you did or did not check. There is nothing particularly significant about which symptoms you did or did not check. Remember, this was an awareness exercise. It gives you an idea, first, of what symptoms to look for and second, it gives you an awareness of symptoms you may have you hadn't really paid much attention to before.

What are your specific symptoms? (The ones you checked "yes" to on your *Symptoms Worksheet.*)

When you look at the symptoms on the list above, what are the two most significant symptoms for you? Write the two most significant symptoms on your *Summary Sheet* under the heading, *"Symptoms to stay aware of."* Write down two for now even if you have more.

Summary Sheet – Symptoms I need to stay aware of:	
First symptom	
Second symptom	

Over time, and as you go through your journey, you may discover the two most significant symptoms you wrote down are pretty much gone. It is then you can go back to the symptoms list and see if another symptom has become the primary one. Knowing your individual symptoms will give you clues as to what to watch for that tell you something is up with you. The *Symptoms Worksheet* is also a great awareness tool to use on a daily or weekly basis to gauge where you are. For this reason, there is an additional copy of the *Symptoms Worksheet* for you to copy for your personal use in the Appendix.

Looking over your *Symptoms Worksheet*, did you have any new awareness about yourself regarding symptoms? Write any new awareness on the lines below.

_____
_____
_____
_____

Here is another great place for a reminder about acceptance. Keep in mind it is really important for you to *accept* your symptoms. You don't have to like the symptoms but you do have to accept you have them in order to move forward. A huge part of this acceptance is dropping your judgment about whether they are good symptoms or bad symptoms. They are just symptoms. Having an opinion about whether they are good or bad just keeps you focused on your judgment of them rather than making choices about them. There will be more about acceptance and judgment in Chapter 6: *Understanding What is Keeping You Stuck*.

Why is it important for you to know your specific symptoms in order to figure yourself out? When you spot one or more of these symptoms it is a signal for you to look and see what is going on in your life. Only with awareness can you begin to take steps to reclaim what is missing. Remember, awareness is not enough. Awareness gives you the opportunity to make a better choice. Make sure you take the next step. Too many times I have heard a client say, "At least I was aware of it." Awareness is step one, though you must remember to take the next step of making a better choice. Not much is going to change in your life except having a whole lot of awareness if you don't make better choices.

Before you start evaluating the rest of your worksheets, remember this very important concept: **Any _one_ answer to any _one_ question on any _one_ of the forms means nothing.** The worksheets work together; one supports the other and vise versa. The information on *all* the forms must be looked at as a whole in order for it to be meaningful. Actually, it is like an attorney building a case for a client. While individual pieces of evidence can seem important, it is the full picture of all the evidence that proves a case.

You will be using a great deal of what you learned about the subconscious mind as you review the rest of your worksheets. Therefore, it is important to remember the subconscious mind:

- is literal
- does not discern
- records everything
- is able to recall most all information stored in it

Life Awareness Worksheet

Take out your *Life Awareness Worksheet* and *Summary Sheet*. Look at Question 1 on your *Life Awareness Worksheet*. The words and phrases you used to describe your problem will give you evidence as to the underlying reason for your problem when you look at your responses *literally*. Look for words or phrases with words in them like:

life	living
death	stuck
ever since I was born	loss
standstill	block
always	procrastinate
I can't stand to be alone	control
start	stop
beginning	moving forward

Phrases and words like these, that describe Walking Zombie (WZ) or Ponce de Leon behavior (PDL), are important as they come from the subconscious part of your mind. From this point on the abbreviation WZ will be used for Walking Zombie. The abbreviation PDL will be used for Ponce de Leon. Here are some examples of what you are looking for in your responses to the first question:

1. "I have lost interest in life." Possible WZ evidence.

2. "I hate living in this town." Possible WZ evidence.
3. "I am feeling stuck." Maybe birth issue - stuck in birth canal, suggestion of death, possible WZ.
4. "Loss of emotion." Possible WZ evidence. Dead people don't feel.
5. "I'm afraid to tell my friends I don't want to do something." Possible PDL--possible child/adolescent behavior.
6. "My life has always been hectic." Always takes you back to birth. Hectic can be proof of life to the subconscious. Possible WZ evidence.
7. "I am at a standstill in my life. I don't feel like doing anything." Possible birth canal issue. Dead people don't feel. Possible WZ evidence.
8. "I have blockages all over." Maybe birth. Possible WZ evidence.
9. "I can't stand being alone." Possible PDL/Walking Zombie evidence.

Review your response to Question 1 on the *Life Awareness Worksheet* very carefully. While you may not have answered *exactly* like the examples, look for similar words or phrases in your response. Did you use any words or phrases that give you some evidence you might have WZ or PDL issues? If you did, write the significant words and phrases you used in your response to this first question on your *Summary Sheet* under the heading, *"Significant Words and Phrases."*

Summary Sheet – Symptoms I need to stay aware of:	
1. First symptom	
2. Second symptom	

Significant Words and Phrases:	
Ex. <u>Stuck, I hate living in this town.</u>	

Look at Question 2 on your *Life Awareness Worksheet*. Just like in Question 1, you will be looking for words and phrases that give you evidence of WZ or PDL issues. If you find any, add them to the list you have already started on your *Summary Sheet* under the heading, *"Significant Words and Phrases."*

Summary Sheet – Symptoms I need to stay aware of:	
1. First symptom	
2. Second symptom	

Significant Words and Phrases:	
Ex. <u>Stuck, I hate living in this town.</u>	
Ex. <u>It started when</u>	

Starting now, you are going to track all numbers you have on your worksheets. Numbers are important throughout this whole process. Many times they will correspond with significant ages in your life or you may begin to see a pattern in your life around numbers. For example, you may see a pattern of changing jobs, or homes or relationships every five years. Keeping track of significant dates can help prepare you for the upcoming anniversaries you will learn about in the Coil Theory in Chapter 5. It is important

> *for you to know it doesn't matter whether you are accurate or inaccurate about the exact date or age. What is important is, as you go along, you track all numbers on all your worksheets.*

Again, look at Question 2 on your *Life Awareness Worksheet*. Did you use any numbers in your response? For example, "5 years ago," or "since I was 3." If you used any numbers in your response, record them on your *Summary Sheet* under the heading, *"Number/Event."* You may or may not be able to tie all your numbers to an event at first, but be patient; you may find the connection as you continue to work through your worksheets.

Summary Sheet – Symptoms I need to stay aware of:	
1. First symptom	
2. Second symptom	
Significant Words and Phrases:	
Ex. <u>Stuck, I hate living in this town.</u>	
Ex. <u>It started when</u>	
Number/Event	
Ex. <u>5 yrs. old</u>	

Hint: Many people will use the phrase, "For as long as I can remember," in response to Question 2. Most people can remember back to around age 3. If you used this phrase, record age 3 on your *Summary Sheet* under the heading, *"Number/Event."*

Summary Sheet – Symptoms I need to stay aware of:	
1. First symptom	
2. Second symptom	
Significant Words and Phrases:	
Ex. <u>Stuck, I hate living in this town.</u>	
Ex. <u>It started when</u>	
Number/Event	
Ex. <u>5 yrs. old</u>	
Ex. <u>age 3 "for as long as I can remember"</u>	

Question 3 on your *Life Awareness Worksheet* is actually a group of questions related to your job or career. You are looking for any words or phrases that give you a hint you may have some WZ or PDL behaviors going on in your life. For example, "I hate my job," might indicate a piece of you dies every time you go to work. "I just don't want to work," might indicate some PDL thoughts or behaviors. If you have these or similar responses, record them on your *Summary Sheet* under the heading, *"Significant Words and Phrases."*

Look at Question 4 on your *Life Awareness Worksheet*. Record every number you used to answer the Life Scale questions on your *Summary Sheet* under the *"Numbers/Events"* heading. Again, you may not be able to tie the number to any particular event right now but record the numbers anyway. If you had a minus number, record that number as well.

Summary Sheet – Symptoms I need to stay aware of:	
1. First symptom	
2. Second symptom	
Significant Words and Phrases:	
Ex. <u>Stuck, I hate living in this town.</u>	
Ex. <u>It started when</u>	
Number/Event	
Ex. <u>5 yrs. old</u>	
Ex. <u>age 3 "for as long as I can remember"</u>	
Ex. <u>-7 on life scale</u>	

Go to Question 5 on your *Life Awareness Worksheet* and pay very close attention to your response. Remember, everything that has ever happened to you is recorded in the subconscious part of your mind, so your *exact* answer is especially important on this question.

If you answered, "yes," there is a pretty good chance a birth event is where your issue began.

If you did respond "yes," record a zero on your *Summary Sheet* under the heading, *"Numbers and Events"* followed by the note, "possible birth trauma."

If you answered, "I don't know," "Not that I've been told" or "I don't think so," be suspicious there may have been something going on you were not consciously aware of.

If you answered with one of those responses, record a zero on your *Summary Sheet* under the heading, *"Numbers and Events"* followed by the note, "possible birth issue."

If you answered, "no," it is less likely birth or before is the beginning of your issue.

However, if you know your mother was having any kind of difficulty when she was pregnant with you, either physically or emotionally, record a negative zero on your *Summary Sheet* under the heading, *"Numbers/Event"* followed by the note "possible birth issue."

Now go to Question 6 on your *Life Awareness Worksheet*. Again, the numbers are very significant so make sure to record them, with a brief description of the event, under the *"Numbers/Events"* heading on your *Summary Sheet*. If you don't know the exact age of a childhood disease, chicken pox for example, but know it was in grade school, enter it on your *Summary Sheet* under *"Numbers/Events"* with the note it occurred in grade school. If it occurred in preschool, you would enter the disease with the note it occurred in preschool and so on.

Summary Sheet – Symptoms I need to stay aware of:	
1. First symptom	
2. Second symptom	
Significant Words and Phrases:	
Ex. <u>Stuck, I hate living in this town.</u>	
Ex. <u>It started when</u>	
Number/Event	
Ex. <u>5 yrs. old</u>	
Ex. <u>age 3 "for as long as I can remember"</u>	
Ex. <u>Grade School--Chicken Pox</u>	
Ex. <u>-7 on life scale</u>	

It is important to understand children experience illness very differently than mature adults. Children don't have the ability to reason about the seriousness of their illness. An illness that feels life-threatening to a child may be relatively insignificant to an adult. How you experience an illness continues to affect you from the age at which you had the illness.

Try to remember what you were told about being sick, especially if it was a WZ suggestion such as, "She may not make it," or "He is going to be lucky to pull through this." Look for anything in the comments that may have been made to you that gives you evidence of WZ or PDL issues. Sometimes an illness, or perhaps what was said to you during that illness, can be the reason you are stuck at that age.

Now go to your *Life Awareness Worksheet* and review your responses to Question 7 and, again, record any numbers under the *"Number/Event"* section of your *Summary Sheet* with a note of the event. For example, age 15, hospitalized for mono. Remember to also look for, and note, any words or phrases you used that can give you evidence of WZ or PDL issues and record them on your *Summary Sheet* under the heading, *"Significant Words and Phrases."*

Consider these questions when you are looking for WZ evidence in your response to Question 7.

1. ***Were you left alone in the hospital? If you were, consider you may have felt abandoned, which could be an emotional WZ suggestion.***

2. ***What kind of anesthesia were you given for the surgery? Local anesthesia has less implication for a WZ suggestion than general anesthesia. General anesthesia is as close to dying as you can come without really dying. Think about***

> *it. They breathe for you, you feel nothing, you remember nothing, you have no control over when or if you regain consciousness. This is definitely a WZ suggestion to your subconscious mind. See Chapter 3, Basic Concepts.*

Now look at Question 8 on your *Life Awareness Worksheet*.

> *What you were told about your condition and what you were told about your prognosis can be a death suggestion. It may be your condition is not necessarily life threatening but may mean you have to give up something you love, which would be a loss, a death of something. For example, you may love to sky dive but your heart condition will no longer allow you to do so.*

Record any WZ death suggestions you discovered in your response to Question 8 under *"Significant Words and Phrases"* on your *Summary Sheet*.

Go to your *Life Awareness Worksheet* and begin your review of Question 9. By now you understand the importance of numbers, so make sure you record all of them, along with a note about the traumatic event on your *Summary Sheet* under the heading, *"Number/Event."*

> *Remember what is important here is whether or not the event was traumatic to YOU. It doesn't matter what anyone else thinks. If it was traumatic to you, then it's significant to you and your journey. Looking back at an event gives your brain*

time to kick in and make it all okay, or at the very least, logical. How something affected you at the time it happened, at the age it happened, is how it is stored in the subconscious part of your mind. It is important to keep this in mind and not minimize something that happened to you as a child or adolescent.

Question 10 deals with the spiritual death possibility of the WZ.

Spiritual WZ is more subtle because most people don't think of guilt as a death suggestion. However, many people have been taught if you commit enough sins, enough times you will go to hell. In fact, many have been taught if you commit some sins, even if only once, you will go to hell. Hell is the ultimate punishment, the death of your soul. Guilt implies punishment. With each piece of guilt you have, a piece of you dies. Yes, this piece of you can be reclaimed. Because guilt is always spiritual death on a subconscious level, it is important you are aware of your guilt and take steps to rid yourself of it and reclaim that piece of life.

Although you may not have a specific number associated with your guilt, guilt is definitely an event to record on your *Summary Sheet* under the heading, *"Number/Event."* An associated number may or may not come to you later.

Go to Question 11 on your *Life Awareness Worksheet* and consider what you may have given up or lost in order to achieve your success. If you find you have given up something important to you or lost something important to you, record this on your *Summary Sheet* along with a date, if possible.

Ask yourself if, in your success, you were trying to prove something. Ask yourself if the success was something you wanted or if it was something someone else wanted for you. Your answer to either of these questions may provide you with hints or evidence of PDL or WZ issues.

Question 12 is an awareness question intended to help you understand that trying to keep something hidden may block you from something you need to see in order to reclaim your life. You don't have to announce whatever it is to the whole world. It is important you acknowledge, embrace and accept whatever it is, at least to yourself. "I don't want to think about it," or "It's done and over with," can keep you stuck.

For now, you are finished with your *Life Awareness Worksheet*. Set it aside and take out your *Words and Phrases Worksheet*.

Words and Phrases Exercise

The purpose of the *Words and Phrases Exercise* is to confirm or deny the information you learned about yourself through reviewing and analyzing your *Life Awareness Worksheet*. Using the information below, look and see where you can confirm the information from your *Life Awareness Worksheet*. Make a note on your *Summary Sheet* next to the items you have confirmed. In addition to confirming the information already on your *Summary Sheet*, you may also learn completely new information or have some additional awareness from your *Words and Phrases Exercise*. Make sure you add any new information to your *Summary Sheet*.

Answer the following questions as honestly and completely as you can. Following each question is a brief explanation of how you might interpret your answer. Remember to look at all your answers literally. The following are some general observations to be aware of on your *Words and Phrases Exercise*.

1. Did you print or use cursive? _____

   Children print. Some adults will say they print so you can read their writing and while that may be true on the conscious level, it can still be a possible indication of some PDL issues. Just observe. Remember, one answer or behavior by itself means very little.

2. Did you use pencil, pen, crayon or marker? _____

   Generally, children use markers and crayons. If you used markers or crayons it might indicate some PDL issues. Some may explain they used crayons because it was the only thing they had. Okay. They still used crayons and it might just add another small piece of evidence indicating possible PDL issues. By the way, having an explanation for almost everything can also indicate a PDL issue only more adolescent than child.

3. Did you answer with the first thought or idea that came up? Or did you think it through and try to figure it out?

_____

Maybe you wanted to make sure you had the *"right"* answer. Maybe you wanted to look good. Again, this might give evidence of PDL issues or it may be a hint of some low self-worth issues.

4. Did you have an emotional reaction to any of the words or phrases? _____. If you did, which one was it and what was your reaction? Was there any WZ or PDL evidence in your emotional response?

_____
_____
_____
_____

5. Were there any words or phrases you left blank? _____ Leaving one or two blank may be insignificant. More than that, it will serve you to see how all those blanks are related or fit together.

6. Did any of your answers surprise you? If yes, which ones? Why did they surprise you?

_____
_____
_____
_____
_____

7. Did you learn anything new about yourself from this exercise? ____ If yes, what?

_____
_____
_____
_____
_____

Just like you did with the *Life Awareness Worksheet,* look for these words: life, death, living, stuck, loss, standstill, block, always, procrastinate, control, start, stop, any number, beginning, it all started when, etc.

Also look for beliefs, rules and opinions in your responses. For example, "life is hard," "there must be an easier way" or "everyone should be kind." Breaking your rules, beliefs and opinions can indicate some WZ issues in that breaking them could be spiritual or emotional pieces of you dying. Having rigid rules and beliefs can also indicate some PDL issues.

Here are some insights on some specific words and phrases to look for on your *Words and Phrases Exercise*:

Number 7 and 8: Both of these take you back to birth and possibly before and might confirm that is where an issue began for you.

Number 9: Death suggestion, WZ. *Feeling* like dying is still a death suggestion even if you did not physically die.

Number 11: Because your subconscious mind is literal, subconsciously you would have to be just like whoever you said you were like. What if the person you said you were just like is dead or ill or a pain in the butt? Subconsciously you would have to have some WZ, be ill and be a pain in the butt. Remember, what we believe subconsciously shows up in our behavior. Also look and see what pieces of yourself you are killing off, or giving away, to be whoever you said you are like?

Number 13: Most likely you answered with an event and this may confirm where the issue consciously began. The "real" beginning of an issue is not usually conscious, such as in a birth trauma.

Number 15: Most common response is "life." People tend to think it is just their mind playing opposites. This is not true. The "life" response shows the subconscious mind's confusion between life and death. When you have had pieces of you die but you are still physically alive it will naturally cause confusion in the subconscious part of your mind because there are parts of you alive and parts of you that have died off.

Number 16: It is important to know who the person is that you don't want to disappoint, beyond yourself. What happens within you when you disappoint someone is important as well. A common response to number sixteen is "anyone." If it is really important to you to not disappoint anyone and you do, a piece of you at some level dies. You are bound to disappoint somebody sometime. That is a lot of WZ. The "anyone" response can also be a matter of people pleasing, which would indicate a PDL issue.

Number 22: Most popular answer is "Who am I?" This can be a PDL response because children are in the process of discovering who they really are. This response can also explain the feeling of frustration and confusion about your life. It is difficult to reclaim your life and live it the way you want when you don't know who you are or if you are trying to be something, or someone, you are not.

Fill in your *Summary Sheet* as completely as possible from the information you learned from your *Words and Phrases Exercise*. Make sure you have noted what items you have confirmed. Also make sure you have included any new information or awareness you learned from your *Words and Phrases Exercise*.

For now, you are finished with your *Words and Phrases Exercise* so set it aside and take out your *Tree Exercise*.

The Tree Exercise

Once you have completed as much information as you can from your *Words and Phrases Exercise,* go to your *Tree Exercise.* Using the information below, check your tree and see where you can confirm the information from your *Life Awareness Worksheet.* Make a note on your *Summary Sheet* next to the items you have confirmed. You may also learn new information or have some additional awareness from your *Tree Exercise.* Make sure you add any new information to your *Summary Sheet.*

The *Tree Exercise* is very subjective. The age lines you drew are to give you an indication of an estimated time frame where there were significant events in your life. This exercise will help you to confirm ages and events in your life that were significant.

Answer the following questions as honestly and completely as you can. Following each question is a brief explanation of how you might interpret your answer. Remember to look at all your answers literally.

1. What kind of a tree did you draw? Was it a stick tree, a Christmas tree, a tall strong tree or a tall thin tree? _____

    What are the thoughts, reasons or explanations you have about the kind of tree you drew?

    _____
    _____
    _____
    _____
    _____

Now, look literally at the tree you drew. How is this tree symbolic of you in general? (sharp, prickly, blossoming, etc.)

_____
_____
_____
_____

2. How detailed did you make your tree? Lots of branches or not? Leaves, no leaves? Full and blossoming or barren?

_____
_____
_____
_____

3. Any knots in the tree? _____ Many times the location of the knots and other markings on the tree will be around the age of a significant event in your life.

4. Is the tree straight, crooked, balanced? Are you straight and rigid in your life? How well balanced is your life?

_____
_____
_____
_____

5. Did you draw outside the space provided or did you stay exactly in the space provided? _____.

    Do you make sure you operate inside the box in your life or do you play outside the box in your life?

    _____
    _____
    _____
    _____

6. Does your tree have roots? _____

    How deep do they go? _____

    Do you have a solid foundation you have built your life on?

    _____
    _____
    _____
    _____

Carry this a bit farther and spend some time examining and defining exactly what foundation you do have in your life.

_____
_____
_____
_____
_____

7. Did you put other things around the tree, like flowers or grass?

_____
_____
_____
_____
_____

If you did put other things around your tree, it can be an indication of other things going on around your birth. It can also be an indication you have a tendency to "pretty up" events and situations in your life and not look at reality. Is it completely barren around your tree? _____ Maybe you need to take time in your life for some fun and genuinely pretty things.

8. Is there anything around your tree like a sun, clouds or birds?

   _____

   Again, are you "prettying things up" or are you taking time in your life for beauty and fun?

   _____
   _____
   _____
   _____

9. What did you use to draw your tree?

   _____

   Crayons or markers may indicate some PDL stuff or, it may indicate you like color and excitement in your life. Did you use a pencil? Maybe you leave room to make mistakes and do it again. Or not. Using a pen might indicate rigidity and not leaving room for errors. Or not.

10. Is your tree in black and white or color? _____ You may love color in your life or you may like to keep it really simple. Or maybe the lack of color is about WZ issues.

11. Did your tree branch out?

_____

Maybe it wasn't the kind of tree that branches out. Notice your approximate age when the tree started branching out, if it did. Many times it will be close to an age where you had a significant event in your life.

If your tree splits and branches out many times, it might signify the times in your life when you added another element to your life or times when you began growing in yet another direction.

12. At what ages did your lines occur?

_____

Pay attention to where your age lines are. Many times these lines will roughly correspond to significant ages and events in your life and can possibly confirm WZ or PDL symptoms beginning or getting worse at those ages.

Now go to your *Summary Sheet* and include any information from your *Tree Exercise* that supports the information you already have there. For example, were any of your WZ or PDL issues confirmed by any of the information you received from your tree? If there were, make a note next to the particular issue on your *Summary Sheet*. If you learned anything new about yourself from your *Tree Exercise,* make sure you make a note on your *Summary Sheet*. For example, you may have learned you are more rule-bound or more open and free in your thinking and actions than you realized.

Summary Sheet

Take out your *Summary Sheet* and notice at the very bottom of the sheet is a section called, *"Important Dates with Possible Anniversary Effects."* Now, look at the *"Number/Event"* section. You are going to use the information in the *"Number/Event"* section to fill in the *"Important Dates with Possible Anniversary Effects"* section. Write in any date that is especially important for you to pay attention to so you can be better prepared for possible issues around that date. For example, if you had a birth trauma, you would put your birthday on one of those lines. You may want to put the date of the death of someone close to you on another one of those lines. This section will then serve as a great reminder to you to stay especially aware around these dates and watch out for a possible increase in frequency or intensity of your specific symptoms.

Summary Sheet – Symptoms I need to stay aware of:	
1. First symptom	
2. Second symptom	
Significant Words and Phrases:	
Ex. <u>Stuck, I hate living in this town.</u>	
Ex. <u>It started when</u>	
Number/Event	
Ex. <u>5 yrs. old</u>	
Ex. <u>age 3 "for as long as I can remember"</u>	
Ex. <u>Grade School--Chicken Pox</u>	

Ex. -7 on life scale	
Important Dates/Possible Anniversary Effects	
Ex. Birthday	

Now, put away the *Self-Assessment* forms you have been using in this chapter. Keep your *Summary Sheet* in front of you and notice the wonderful outline you have created. When you look at your *Summary Sheet* you see you have a clearer picture of yourself. You have an idea of what behaviors to look for and you know your two main symptoms that tell you something is unhealthy.

At this point, by reviewing your *Summary Sheet,* you can see what event may have been the beginning of some of your issues. When you know what this event was, you have the opportunity to do the work to heal and grow from that event. From your *Summary Sheet* you will also be able to tell what events made the issues worse for you and, again, knowing this, you have the opportunity to do the work to heal and grow from those events. Keep in mind some of these events or issues you will be able to work through yourself and, for other issues, you may need or want to seek professional guidance. As you work through the issues you will be reclaiming more and more pieces of yourself and, as you do, you will have more of you with which to live your life more fully. Use your *Summary Sheet* as an outline to guide yourself in taking the steps to reclaim your life.

You have looked at a lot of the things in your life. You have a much better understanding of what makes you tick and why you are the way you are. This information is ***not*** for you to use as an excuse.

Neither is it for you to use against yourself. This information is for you to use as a guide towards healing, growing and stepping more fully into your life. Now you have a great deal of useful information you can use to begin to live the life you love. Please keep in mind, there is still more.

Summary Sheet Exercise

Symptoms I need to stay aware of:

1. _____
   _____
   _____
   _____
   _____
   _____
   _____

2. _____
   _____
   _____
   _____
   _____
   _____
   _____

Significant Words and Phrases:

_____
_____
_____
_____
_____

Number/Event:

_____
_____
_____
_____

Important Dates with Possible Anniversary Effects:

_____
_____
_____
_____

WARNING! Now that you have gone through the process this far and completed the *Summary Sheet,* you may discover you have more awareness in general. You may recognize things in other people you have learned on your journey towards figuring yourself out. At times, it may seem like you are seeing messed-up people all over the place. Please stop yourself from pointing out other people's stuff to them. They are not asking you to show them where they are messed up and the likelihood of them appreciating your insight is slim, unless they are really codependent. Bottom line is, if you have an insight you want to share with them, ask their permission first. If they say, "No, I don't want to hear what you have to say," let it go. It's none of your business! Yes, even if it is your best friend, a parent or your adult child. Please keep your insight to yourself. However, if they come back to you later and want to talk with you about your insight, it is absolutely okay to set a healthy time to do so.

You *can* use your awareness and insight into others as an opportunity to learn and practice compassion for and non-judgment of others. A really great way to practice this is to ask, "What could have happened to me that would cause me to behave that way?" It is not about making excuses for poor behavior. It *is* about having more understanding for yourself and others.

Additional Resources for Chapter 4

The effects of a possible birth trauma were mentioned in this chapter. If you would like more information about this concept, contact the American Academy of Medical Hypnoanalysts or go to www.aamh.com and order the articles on birth from their store.

The Way It Works

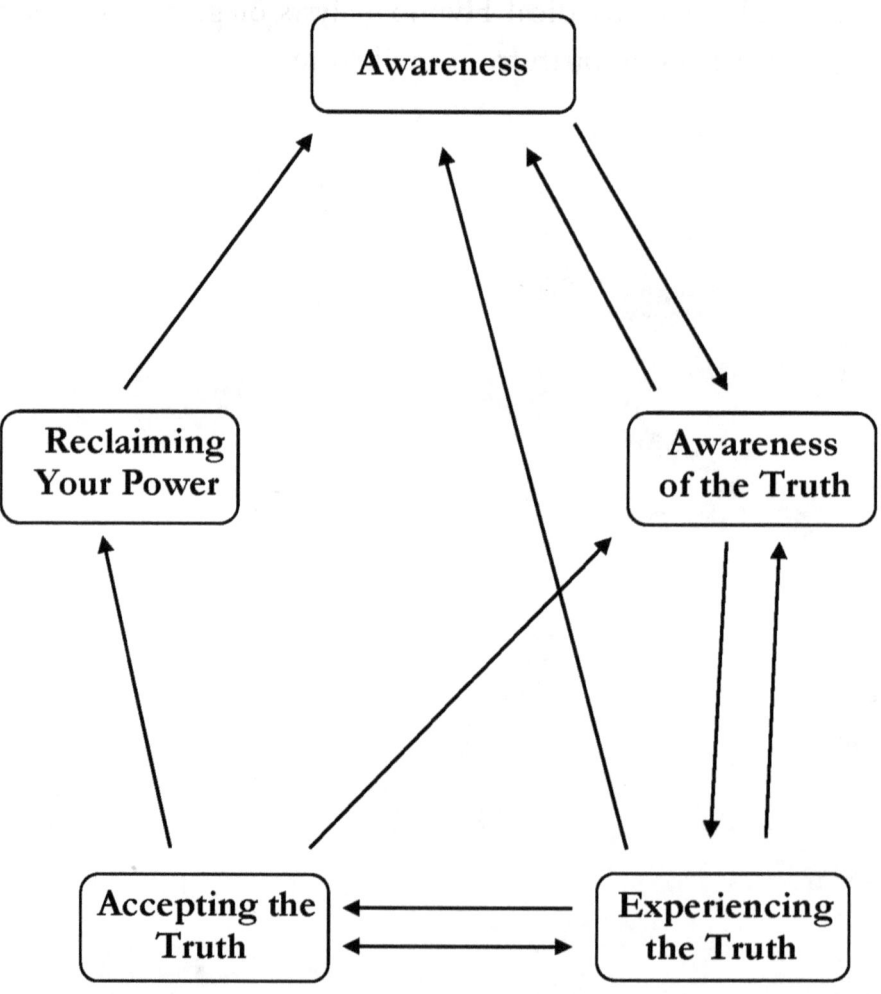

CHAPTER 5

Your Process and What to Expect

In this chapter you will learn about the process you will be going through and some of the things you will experience while you go through the process. You will also begin to understand, through the Coil Theory, why it sometimes feels like you are right back where you started. Becoming familiar with Elisabeth Kubler-Ross' *Five Stages of Grief* will help you understand some of the feelings and symptoms of grief you may experience in your process of losing your issues and reclaiming your life. You will also learn the value and necessity of practice, practice, practice. Remember the "butt on the bench and the fingers on the keyboard" from Chapter 3.

The Way It Works

When I introduce this topic sometimes I get the question, "The way what works?" The answer is, "Reclaiming your life and getting what you want from it." This includes reclaiming every single part of you on every level; physically, mentally, emotionally and spiritually.

There are five main stages everyone goes through to reclaim their power and thus begin to live the life they love. As the diagram shows, in your process, it is normal to bounce back and forth between the steps. It is not a straight 1, 2, 3, 4, 5 journey. You will go back and forth between the steps frequently until you get it. It has to do with the experiencing and accepting stages. Some people have difficulty staying in the experiencing stage long enough for it to be complete. They may *think* they have completed the experiencing stage and are ready to move on to acceptance but many times they are not. They may have to go through the experiencing stage more than once or twice in order to truly move on to the acceptance stage.

Yes, you can be retriggered! You are retriggered when something happens to send you back into an old behavior or illusion. Even when you think you have gone through all the stages and reclaimed your power, it is possible for you to be retriggered either by an anniversary effect or a new, but similar, event.

The first stage in the Reclaiming Your Life Process is the *Awareness Stage*. The awareness I am speaking of here is the funny feeling that says, "There's just something that's not quite right." Filling out the *Life Awareness Worksheet* and the other worksheets in Chapter 2 may have stirred up that feeling for you. At other times, it's just a feeling of unease. You can't define it and you can't necessarily name it. But there it is. This is the beginning of the realization you have a really big, honking illusion. In other words, you begin to suspect things are not what they seem or the way you thought they were. You may even begin to notice you have some of the symptoms described within the *Symptoms Worksheet* in Chapter 2.

- Example: "I always thought I had a close and loving family. But, you know, the last few family holidays just didn't seem to be the same. Maybe it's just me."
- Example: "He says we're fine but something has changed."

Are there things in your life you suspect may not be what they seem? If there are, list them below. (Be sure to include any internal thoughts or beliefs you may have about yourself.)

_____
_____
_____
_____
_____
_____
_____

Stage two is *Awareness of the Truth*. This is the stage where you begin to see the evidence of what is really going on. This is the stage where you begin to see the behaviors you observe don't match what you have believed.

- Example: "Look how Dad is always putting Mom down because she never worked outside the home. Look at how Mom manipulates my sister to get her to run her errands for her. I've never really paid much attention when my brothers always brought a six-pack and two bottles of wine to dinner. Maybe I don't have the close and loving family I thought I did."
- Example: "He is always gone and doesn't have much to say even when he is home."
- Example: "I've always been told I'm dumb. If I'm dumb how could I pass a class with an A?"

Are there places in your life where what you see doesn't match what you have believed or what you have been told? How does what you have been told differ from what you have observed?

_____

_____

_____

_____

_____

_____

_____

A note on stages one and two: ***Awareness is not enough!*** Many times I have had clients say to me, "But at least I was aware of it." That is where they stop. It is great they had the awareness but it's not enough. You need to take the next step and make a healthier choice than you have before. Stopping at the awareness stage will definitely keep you stuck.

Stage three is *Experiencing the Truth* and then dealing with all the feelings and other "stuff" that goes along with really getting it. This means feeling the hurt, the pain, the anger, the disappointment and so on that is involved in what you are seeing. While it can be unpleasant, it is important to remember the only way to really quit feeling and experiencing all the stuff is to go through it. That's right. You have to feel and experience it. Anything less than feeling and experiencing is checking out and going back into stage one or two of the process. This is a great place to bring in the concept of *checking out*.

When you check out you don't have to experience the truth. When you check out you don't have to feel. When you check out it's a pretty good indication there is something going on you don't want to see. Ignoring it, denying it, checking out from it, drinking it away, eating it away, smoking it away, drugging it away, gambling it away or keeping really busy only gives you more grief in the long run and keeps you stuck. Yes, it can be very uncomfortable to go through, but it sure beats the consequences of *not* going through it and staying stuck.

What do you use to check out? Reviewing your *Symptoms Worksheet* may give you some clues in addition to the list above.

_____
_____
_____
_____
_____
_____

Examples of experiencing the truth:

- "When Dad puts Mom down because she never worked outside the home I feel angry and powerless and I want to defend her and tell him to back off."
- "When Mom manipulates my sister to run her errands for her I feel disgusted and I think my sister is really stupid because she falls for it every time."
- "I've never really paid much attention when my brothers bring a six-pack and two bottles of wine to dinner but now I realize after the second bottle of wine they start fighting over everything. How stupid could I be for not having seen it all before? They ruin the meal for everyone and they should be more considerate and think of others beside themselves."

Sometimes it might just be a matter of feeling and experiencing the turmoil and anger, feeling and experiencing the judgment and feeling and experiencing the upset stomach and rapid heartbeat.

Stage four is the stage in which you *Accept the Truth.* This means you have no more energy or attachment to the issue than you do to the fact the sun rises in the east and water runs downhill. You no longer judge the situation or really have any feelings about it period. It just is. Stay aware during this stage especially if you have no feelings at all about the issue. Make sure you haven't checked out from the situation which could be why you don't have any feelings about it. Practice, practice, practice checking in with yourself on a regular basis. This is where the *Stay in Touch* exercise can come in handy. When you accept a situation, you are aware of the situation and you take care of yourself in the situation. You just have no attachment to it.

Take some time now and go back to your *Figuring Yourself Out Summary Sheet.* List any of the symptoms or events you are having a difficult time accepting.

_____

_____

_____

_____

_____

_____

Stage five is *Reclaiming Your Power*. Reclaiming your power means you are moving on with your life and are no longer using your energy on something that is done and over with and you have no control over.

Unfortunately, this is not an automatic step. You have to actively choose in every moment, over and over again, to reclaim your power. That is the practice, practice, practice part.

In reclaiming your power you are making a mature and empowered choice about how you want to deal with the situation. You can never pretend the situation didn't happen, because it did happen. To pretend it didn't is denial and you will very likely throw yourself right back into the state of illusion you were in before you began this journey.

What does understanding how the *Reclaim Your Life Process* works have to do with figuring yourself out? When you understand it is a process and you will go through several steps, this process gives you guidelines you can use to keep yourself on track and check on your progress. Understanding you will move back and forth between the stages can give you some reassurance you are not really back to square one. It is only part of the reclaiming process.

The Coil Theory

Have you ever felt like you were back to square one? Do you ever feel like you are dealing with the same issues over and over and over and over and over again? Well, the fact of the matter is, you may be back to square one sometimes. The same issues do continue to come up over and over again until you have gone through *The Way It Works Process*, perhaps more than once.

We live in a linear thinking and experiencing world. Linear thinking requires us to see things as moving forward in a straight line, never going back and revisiting what has happened before. So, when you have that back to square one feeling you may think there is something terribly wrong with you. Straight line thinking sets you up for judgment, sets you up for rule making, sets you up for having to be right and sets you up to not be okay with going back and learning where you may have missed something the first time. When you continue to deal with what seems to be the same issue over and over again you may begin to feel you must really be stupid if you aren't getting it by now. Because we live in such a linear world, it is easy to get stuck in linear explanations for everything and when that doesn't make sense you may feel stuck.

Most human growth and development theories rely on the linear way of thinking. Example: First you roll over, then you sit up, then you crawl, then you stand up, then you walk and, finally, you run.

---roll over---sit up---crawl---stand up---walk---run----

The same kind of thinking seems to apply in emotional and mental developmental theories as well. Because of this, it is easy to get stuck in linear explanations for everything. The problem is linear thinking and explanations cannot answer such questions as, "Why am I back to square one?" or "How come I keep dealing with the same issues over and over again?" *The Coil Theory* of growth and development can give understanding to these questions in a way linear explanations cannot.

Study the diagram of a coil. See how it winds around and around itself and always comes back to where it started only on a different level? Think of the beginning of the coil as your beginning, your *birth* day. Each year you circle around and on your first birthday you are back to where you started only on a higher level. The same thing happens your second and third year and every year until you die. So, it is possible that each year your birth experience is retriggered in the subconscious part of your mind. Around one's birthday some may have a pleasant experience and some may have an unpleasant experience. *The Coil Theory* helps to explain why some people dislike their birthday but can't necessarily tell you why. Being aware of why you may dislike your birthday and the possible reasons for it gives you the opportunity to do some healing around your birthday every time it comes up. It is possible for your birthday to become more pleasant and some people have even gotten so far as actually celebrating their birthdays.

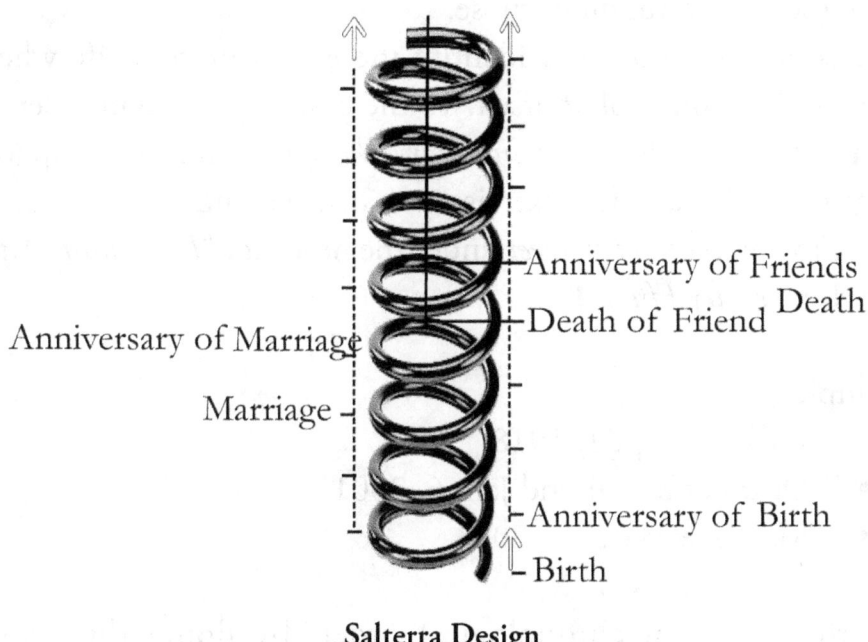

Salterra Design

This same principle holds true for any other significant event in your life. Every year as you come around to the anniversary of that event, the event is retriggered in your mind, only at a different level. All the events in your life are revisited each year, either consciously or subconsciously, regardless if they are pleasant or unpleasant. If you experience a rough time, anxiety or depression at any of your anniversary times, you probably have some healing work to do. Each time you revisit an event you have the opportunity to heal whatever needs to be healed. If you are not aware of this opportunity, you can't possibly take advantage of it. When you are able to take advantage of the opportunity to heal, an initially traumatic event can impact you less and less each year.

What does understanding the *Coil Theory* have to do with figuring yourself out? When you are aware you will revisit situations and have the opportunity to do further healing during that time. Or, you could always celebrate the wonderful on purpose.

Take some time now and identify the events in your life where you need to reclaim a piece of yourself. To the best of your ability identify the date of the event. Revisit your *Summary Sheet* to see if it will help jog your memory. Or, if through this exercise, you discover more anniversary dates, add them to you *Summary Sheet* under the heading, *"Important Dates with Possible Anniversary Effects."*

Example:
- Birthday Sept 1, 1918
- Death of best friend Jan. 6, 2001
- Marriage March 5, 2003

Put the events in chronological order. By doing this, you have created an awareness tool for yourself. With this awareness you can actively begin healing exercises (these will be individual based on the person and the event) several weeks before and several weeks after the event. You would continue this exercise until the event no longer holds a charge for you.

_____

_____

_____

_____

Elisabeth Kubler-Ross' *Five Stages of Grief*

As you are on your journey towards being whole and having the life you want, you will be losing the unhealthy behaviors, thoughts and ideas you have had for a very long time. And, while you are getting rid of them on purpose, you will still grieve their loss and go through the stages of grief for each one to some degree or another. As mentioned before, you will grieve the loss, the death, of your issues. Remember, your subconscious mind is literal and a death is a death is a death. It may seem rather silly, or even stupid, to experience grief over the loss of something that has been unhealthy for you, but it is something that has been a part of your life for probably a very long time and it is still a loss. Remember how your subconscious mind works… a loss is a loss is a loss. Because of this concept, it is important for you to grieve the loss of your unhealthy behaviors, thoughts and ideas just like you would if you lost someone or something important to you.

The stages of grief are the same whether you are grieving the loss of your issues or the loss of a loved one. The Kubler-Ross stages of grief are **denial** ("I don't really need to stop smoking."), **anger** ("It's not fair. Charlie smokes more than I do and he doesn't have chronic bronchitis and pneumonia."), **bargaining** ("Maybe if I just cut down."), **depression** ("I don't feel like doing anything.") and **acceptance** ("I can't smoke. It makes me sick.").

She originally applied these stages to people who were terminally ill but later applied these same stages to any kind of personal loss. Remember, the loss of your unhealthy symptoms is still a loss. Having a basic understanding of Elisabeth Kubler-Ross' *Five Stages of Grief* will support you in understanding what you are going through in your process of reclaiming your life.

Take a few moments now to identify any areas in your life where you are healing and growing and are in the grief process around losing some of your symptoms. Identify where you think you are in the process.

Examples:
- Not enabling others - denial stage ("Just this one time and then she's on her own.")
- Not telling lies - anger stage ("Everybody else lies.")
- Losing weight - bargaining stage ("I'll eat the candy bar now and then go to the gym.")
- Not gossiping - denial stage ("*That's* not really gossip.")

_____
_____
_____
_____

Identify any areas or situations in your life you don't want to deal with and just wish they would go away. You may even tell yourself you are just fine with the way these things are.

_____
_____
_____
_____

The first step in actually dealing with the above issues is to admit and accept where you are with the issue, and that is, "I don't want to deal with it." You may want to refer back to Chapter 2 and the section on knowing where you are starting. When you see a situation you don't want to deal with, ask yourself how it serves you to not deal with it. It doesn't serve you is the answer to the question. Solution…..deal with it!

Keeping in mind the process of *The Way it Works* will support you in understanding that this healing, growing and moving forward stuff is a process with no time limit and no straight lines to your destination. Understanding this process will support you to be patient with yourself through your learning and growing.

Additional Resource for Chapter 5

To learn more about the five stages of grief read *On Death and Dying* by Elisabeth Kubler-Ross, M.D. While this book addresses physical death, it can also be applied to any kind of death, which is what Kubler-Ross herself did in her later work.

CHAPTER 6

Step 4: Understanding What Is Keeping You Stuck

As you are working through the steps to reclaim your life, it may sometimes feel like nothing is really changing for you. You may even feel stuck. On the other hand, you may be rolling along, making progress, doing your thing and, what seems like all of a sudden, the wheels fall off and you're right back stuck wondering what the heck happened. There are many thoughts, beliefs and behaviors that will keep you stuck. Some are subconscious and some are conscious.

It is possible you may be stuck even if you don't feel like you are. Being stuck means you are not moving forward in your life the way you want to or could. While you may not necessarily feel as though you are stuck, it is important to be aware of behaviors that may indicate you are, in fact, stuck. Some of the warning signs in your behavior include:

- Fighting to be right
- Waiting until you feel like it
- Feeling like you shouldn't have to
- I don't want to so I'm not going to
- Beginning your sentences with, "Yeah but…"
- Not wanting to change
- Wanting someone else to change to make it easier for you
- Thinking you have it all figured out

Since it is much easier to get unstuck if you catch the behavior early, it would serve you to check in with yourself daily. Ask yourself if you are experiencing any of the behaviors described above. Keep in mind you may have some stuck symptoms unique to you, so stay aware of those as well.

Once you identify yourself as being stuck or feeling stuck, here are some steps to follow to help you figure out why you might be stuck:

1. Review your *Life Awareness Worksheet* to see if it will trigger any new thoughts or insights. Is it possible you are missing a piece of yourself you were not previously aware of?

2. Double check the list of your specific symptoms to see if any of your symptoms are worse or if you have developed a new symptom. If so, when did the symptom start to get worse and what was happening at that time in your life? It may just be a matter of going back and dealing with an issue you previously overlooked.

3. Have you gone on auto pilot? For example, if you are writing your affirmations or using your check lists without connecting or focusing on what you are doing, you are probably on auto pilot. It is important to really pay attention. If you find yourself on auto pilot, take extra time to re-focus and concentrate on each step you take on your journey.

    What are behaviors or thoughts you need to watch for indicating you might be on auto pilot?

    _____
    _____
    _____
    _____

4. Check and see where you are focusing. Are you focusing on how far you have to go or how hard the process is for you? If so, change your focus. Focus on the progress you have made and celebrate it. If some of the steps on your journey to reclaiming your life seem really difficult, take some time to focus on ways you can make the process more enjoyable, or at least more tolerable.

    What are some healthy ways you can make some of the chores and actions on your journey more enjoyable? Example: Playing music while writing your affirmations.

    _____
    _____
    _____
    _____

5. Ask yourself if you are waiting for permission from someone (including yourself) in order to proceed. For example, if your mother never approved of you pursuing art, there may be a part of you waiting for her to encourage you to go ahead and paint. ***Give yourself permission to paint and go ahead and paint!***

    Waiting for permission is very closely associated with waiting for someone to "get it" or "get you." Accept they are probably not going to get it. They may never get you and they are not going to give you permission. ***You get it, so give yourself permission and move on.*** Remember, you will probably experience some grieving as part of your process of letting go and moving on. Review the stages of grief in Chapter 5.

Who are you waiting for to give you permission to move forward in your life?

_____
_____
_____
_____

Who do you want to "get you" before you move forward in your life?

_____
_____
_____
_____

What do you want to happen before you move forward in your life?

_____
_____
_____
_____

6. Check and see if you are taking things, including you and your life, way too seriously. The world will probably not end if there is a huge dust bunny behind the chair or you bought dessert for dinner instead of making it from scratch. Take a few moments now and

write down ways in which you might be taking things or your life too seriously.

_____
_____
_____
_____

Take as much pressure off yourself as you possibly can and **take your time**. Being in a hurry about anything, including figuring yourself out and reclaiming your life, can cause you to make mistakes which can lead to a whole load of problems. Being in a hurry usually means someone is in destination thinking. They are in a hurry to get to a particular place because *then* they can be happy, relax, golf, write a book, be in a relationship and so on. The problem with destination thinking is there is usually another destination, and then another destination and then another destination, etc. *What* are you in a hurry about?

_____
_____
_____
_____

7. Check and see if you are too close to the situation to see it clearly. Sometimes being stuck is a matter of you being too close to the issue to figure it out. It's the old "you can't see the forest for the trees" trick. If you think this might be the case, check in with a professional to

see if you are missing something. Notice checking in with a friend or family member wasn't suggested. Many times they are too close to you and too close to the issue to see it accurately either. If you think being too close to the situation is a possibility for you, make an appointment with a professional to see if you are missing something.

8. Sometimes people are stuck because there are issues they are trying to deal with they are not qualified to deal with and really cannot handle alone. Nor should they try to handle them alone. If it is possible you have issues you are not qualified or able to handle on your own, be open and willing to seek professional help when necessary.

Are there any issues in your life you suspect you may need to consult a professional about?

_____
_____
_____
_____

Are you willing to consult a professional? _____

If not, why not?

_____
_____
_____
_____

9. Check and see if you are thinking you have this stuff all figured out and you are now ready to go beyond the basics. You want something new or different or better. This may happen when you are getting bored with the foundation work you are doing. So, here's the truth: You can never leave the basics behind. Of course, you can always build on the basics, but you have to keep the basics in place otherwise you are very likely to get stuck.

    The solution is to include something new to make what you are already doing more interesting. Try writing your affirmations in different colors, finding new music to play while you are meditating or use stars or stickers on your check sheets. Bottom line is, sometimes it's just a matter of doing it even if it is boring.

10. Check to see if you are feeling guilty. Better yet, check to see if you *have* guilt as you may have guilt and not necessarily be *feeling* guilty. If you are someone who has shut-down feelings, you wouldn't feel guilty. In fact, that may be one of the reasons why you have shut down your feelings. Point being, guilt implies punishment and what a better way to punish yourself than to keep yourself from moving forward and reclaiming your life. The obvious solution is to forgive yourself. If you are unable to forgive yourself, it is time to ask for help from a professional.

11. Check to see if you are dealing with an issue of feeling entitled. For example, feeling like the world owes you, like you are special, or like you are an exception or you are better than others are all indications of a possible entitlement issue.

Example:
- I shouldn't have to write affirmations.
- I don't need to set goals.
- *Other people* may need to do that.
- I've paid my dues.
- I've put in my time.

12. Ask yourself if you have reverted back to some old ways of thinking or picked up old beliefs or illusions about yourself.

Example:
- I'm stupid.
- I can't write.
- I'm ugly.
- I'm not good at relationships.

13. Above all, the most common reason for people getting stuck is, almost always, because of their

- Judgments
- Opinions
- Beliefs
- Expectations
- Rules

Yes, JOBERs will *always* keep you stuck. They will always keep you stuck because you are so focused on being right and not willing to change, you are unable to see any other way except yours. Being right is so important to some people that being wrong feels like a threat to their very survival, which is why they will fight to be right no matter what the cost.

When we are talking about being judgmental, we are talking about making something or someone right or wrong, good or bad, positive or negative. Situations and people are much easier to deal with if you are not judging them.

Be clear. Being judgmental is very different from using your good judgment. You need to use your good judgment to make healthy choices and decisions in your life. You weigh the pros and cons of a particular situation. You judge what you believe is best of the choices you have. You *can* make those choices without being judgmental.

How are you judgmental in your everyday life? In other words, what situations or people do you judge as good or bad, right or wrong, positive or negative? Make a list on the lines below:

_____
_____
_____
_____
_____
_____

Your opinions and your beliefs are just that. *Your* opinions and beliefs. You might even have a whole bunch of people who agree with you and mountains of research to prove you are right. It is healthy to consider you, all those other people and the research just might be wrong. When you are willing to open yourself to the possibility of being wrong, you also open yourself to all sorts of possibilities for new learning and growth.

Are you willing to look at the possibility you are mistaken about any of your beliefs? Which ones?

_____
_____
_____
_____
_____
_____

Expectations are of your own making. It doesn't necessarily mean anyone else is going to agree with you or care to meet your expectations. Dropping your expectations doesn't mean you have to settle for less or tolerate poor behavior. It does mean you are free to experience and accept what is so and then choose how you are going to respond.

For now, write down one expectation preventing you from moving forward in your life. Continue to write down your expectations as you become aware of them during your journey through this book.

_____

_____

_____

_____

_____

_____

_____

How thick is your rule book? You know the one. The one where, according to you, all the rules people are supposed to follow are written down. All the arbitrary rules you make for yourself are in your personal rule book too. You may not be consciously aware you even have a rule book, but you do. All the rules that have you feel guilty, unworthy, superior, smart, dumb, right, wrong, good, bad, etc. are catalogued and stored in your mind ready to be pulled out at a moment's notice.

A great awareness exercise is to make the rule book you carry around in your head physical. Write down all the rules you expect yourself and others to follow, no matter how seemingly insignificant. Actually print your rule book and keep it with you. Add to it whenever you find yourself faced with another rule. The key here is to remember if you made the rule, or accepted a rule someone else made, you can un-make the rule.

DROP ALL OF YOUR JUDGMENTS, OPINIONS, BELIEFS, EXPECTATIONS AND RULES, THEN LIFE IS A BREEZE.

CHAPTER 7
Steps to Take and Tools to Help You

You've filled out all the forms in Chapter 2. You've studied the basic concepts in Chapter 3. You've used what you learned in Chapter 3 to interpret your responses on the forms you filled out in Chapter 2. You've used the information in Chapter 4 to help you get a clearer picture of your issues, where they started, what made them worse and why you still have them. You have completed your *Summary Sheet* so you have, at the very least, an intellectual understanding of what is going on with you and why. You have gone through Chapter 5 and have a basic understanding of the process you will be going through and some of the things you will experience while you go through your process. So the next question is, "Now what?"

Now your practice really begins. *Now* you begin to reclaim the pieces of yourself you have lost. *Now* you begin the process of healing which enables you to grow beyond your issues. It is important to understand it is, indeed, a process. This process will take time, it will take practice and it will take patience. It will take patience with the process and patience with yourself.

In this chapter are simple steps you can take and basic tools you can use that will support you on your journey to figuring yourself out and transitioning from stuck to star of your life. It is important you choose the steps and the tools that appeal to you the most. However, it is also important to at least try some of the other tools as well. And, try them for a long enough period of time to make an informed and honest decision about whether or not a particular tool is useful to you. **Hint:** Sometimes the ones you dislike the most will give you the most learning and the most support. Please do not try and implement all these tools and steps at once.

Take one tool or step at a time and when you are comfortable with one, add another.

Stay in awareness. The most important thing, and the key, to reclaiming your life is to make sure you *keep* the awareness you have gained by going through the exercises. You've written everything down so you can go back and review any time you want. Want a quick review? Re-read your *Summary Sheet*.

Hint: It will serve you to write in your calendar the anniversary dates you discovered and recorded on your *Summary Sheet*. For example, if it so happens your birthday is a trigger event for you, several weeks before your birthday until several weeks after your birthday use this affirmation twice daily: "I was born alive and free. I am a child of God and the Universe with every right in the world to be here." Say this affirmation aloud AND write it slowly and deliberately.

Use this technique with all your anniversaries. Find or write an appropriate affirmation for each situation and begin to use it several weeks before the anniversary until several weeks after the anniversary. The affirmations serve to help you re-program your mind but they also may bring up unresolved *stuff* around the anniversary. If this happens, you have an opportunity to do some healing around the event.

Just take a step. Almost any step will do. Move! Movement builds momentum. **Stop** trying to figure out which step is the *right* one or the *best* one. This will only keep you stuck in inaction or in overwhelm. Perhaps one of the easiest places to start is with an affirmation. What affirmation do you start with? You can build it around an anniversary as suggested above or you can refer to your *Life Awareness Form* and look at your answer to the very first question. From that answer pick one of your primary concerns or issues and begin using an affirmation about the particular concern or issue.

For example, if one of your issues is anxiety, you may start to overcome that issue by using the affirmation, "I am calm and relaxed." Using the affirmation will, at the very least, help you to begin to re-program your subconscious mind. There is more detailed information in Chapter 10 about affirmations and how to write and use them.

You can also refer to your *Summary Sheet*. It will remind you of the issues and the incidents you want or need to heal. Refer to any of the exercises or experiences you completed earlier in the book. They are all geared to "bring stuff up" and bringing stuff up gives you another opportunity to heal.

By the way, an affirmation that will serve you to use on a regular basis is, "Dear God, Great Spirit, Universe, please give me accurate awareness."

Develop a self-care check sheet. Using a daily self-care check sheet will support you in remembering to take better care of yourself. This list will help you eliminate the "I forgot" excuse. "I forgot to take my vitamins," "I forgot to write my affirmations," and so on.

Use a schedule. You may already use an appointment schedule for your work. If you do, expand that schedule to include your personal time. Schedule time for you to include not only your needs but also your wants. If you are one of those "I don't have time" people, begin to make the time by putting time in the schedule just for you. Schedule you time when you are fairly confident you will allow nothing to take that time away from you. Some people start with finding five minutes for themselves during the day. If five minutes a day is where you need to start, give yourself permission to have it be okay to start with *only* five minutes a day. Then make sure you are increasing the time for yourself on a regular basis.

Please keep in mind a self-care check sheet and a schedule are for you to use as a guide. Many times those new to using these two tools will use them as a way to beat themselves up if they don't accomplish everything on the sheet. Remember, these tools are guidelines and learning techniques to help you on your journey.

Take some time to **journal** each day. Before you completely dismiss the idea as something you don't want to do or you've done it before, take a moment and consider the following. Journaling is a safe way to express your feelings, ideas and emotions. Some like to save what they have written and use it to reflect on periodically. Others want to make sure what they write is safe and will destroy what they have written each day. The whole idea is about beginning to express you in a safe way. Journaling each day does not mean you have to write two or three pages or even two or three paragraphs. Make a commitment to write *something* each day, even if it is only one sentence like, "I don't feel like writing in this darn journal today." Sometimes you might write just one word that says it all for you on a particular day. The important thing is to get into the habit of writing something every day so on the days you want or need to express something, you have the habit in place.

Use A WOW Book. A client came to a session one day with a small journal book in her hand. She had been frustrated because it seemed to her she had to learn the same things over and over and over. She was discouraged because some of her great awareness' (her WOWs) seemed to disappear shortly after a session. Her solution was to start what she called her WOW Book!

In order to understand the value of this tool, let me tell you one more thing about the subconscious mind. **Anytime anyone has any kind of a problem their subconscious mind believes they need the problem for some kind of survival.** Yes, there is a whole lot more to this than we are going to go into here. But, for now use a WOW book. When you get your insights, your WOWs, which can help you get rid of your problem, your subconscious mind may say, "No way! If you let go of this problem, you will die at some level. It is better, it is survival to keep the problem rather than die." See Chapter 3 to review the subconscious mind. Forgetting your insights, your ah-ha moments, is the mind's way of protecting the scared you.

Writing your WOWs in your book does a couple of things for you. First, it has you remember when your mind would have you forget. Second, each time you re-read the insight it reinforces the memory in your mind and it reinforces the power of the insight for you. It will give you that new insight, WOW feeling, each time you read it. Third, with repetition, the new awareness becomes a permanent part of your new belief system. Remember to allow the feelings and experience of the WOW to come forward along with the memory. In this way you are getting the most learning.

There are many other tools you can use to keep yourself on the path to figuring yourself out and moving from stuck to star of your life. Three of these tools are so important they needed an entire chapter to themselves.

BE PATIENT… People hear half of what is said, they understand half of that, they agree with half of that, they remember half of that and they get one-half of that.
~Anonymous~

CHAPTER 8
Clean and Clear Communication

Lack of clean and clear communication is the cause of most of the problems people have with family, friends, co-workers, bosses, spouses, partners and children. One of the most important things to remember about communication is **every single human being in this world wants to be heard** and this includes you. It is part of being human.

Communication is an interaction with another person in which you exchange thoughts, ideas, perhaps even feelings and emotions. There are two parts to communication. Speaking and listening.

Being a Mature and Empowered Speaker

Let's begin by looking at what it takes to be a clean and clear speaker. The first step is to know exactly what you want to get out of the conversation. First of all, you must be clear and clean within yourself before you can communicate cleanly and clearly with the other person. A question to ask yourself is, "What are the results I want from this conversation?" Possible answers to that question: "I just want to be heard," "I want them to change their behavior," "I want them to agree with me" or "I want them to tell me I am right." Set the drama and emotion aside for the moment and make sure you are totally clear and honest with yourself about what you want from the conversation before you even start it.

By the way, setting the drama and emotion aside, looking at the facts and becoming totally clear and honest with yourself is what is known as having an intellectually honest conversation with yourself.

Some other things to think about when speaking:

1. Hinting and manipulation is not clean and clear communication. In fact, hinting and manipulation are two of the biggest causes of messed-up communication. Just come out and say what you need to say! Just come out and ask what you want to know. This may take practice for those of you who have been using hinting and manipulation to get what you want.

   Take some time now to look at your communication skills. Think back over situations or conversations you have had in the last three months where you wanted to have the person you were talking to change the way they did something or where you wanted them to do something for you. On the lines below, write some notes about what you notice in your communication in those situations. Did you hint, hoping they would get the hint and change their behavior or offer to do what you wanted them to do? Or, did you say what you needed to say cleanly and clearly?

   _____
   _____
   _____
   _____
   _____

How could you have said it better?

_____

_____

_____

_____

Now you have more awareness about how you communicate a request. Keep some notes on your communication over the next three days and see what else you notice in your communication.

_____

_____

_____

_____

2. Just because someone can repeat back to you exactly what you said does not mean they "get it." Another part of this is just because someone says they got it doesn't mean they really got it. They may have gotten it intellectually (remember helmet understanding from Chapter 3) but it doesn't necessarily mean they've experienced or really understood what you said.

3. Beware of being "on too long." Sometimes it is really hard to recognize this in yourself. Make sure you say what you need to say in as short a

time as possible *while still getting the message across*. You may lose your audience quickly if you give the history, with the table of contents and bibliography before getting to the point. If it is simply a matter of wanting to be heard, warn the person ahead of time so they are prepared to take the time needed for you to get it all out.

If you think you might be on too long, ask yourself if you are really just trying to convince someone of something. You give them all the possible reasons why they should do what you want them to do or think the way you want them to think. Of course, be aware when someone else is on too long and what they may be trying to "sell" you.

Observe your personal communications during the next week. Write down your observations to these questions, "Do I go on and on and on and on and on or am I clear and to the point?" "Am I open to seeing the real answer to this question?"

_____
_____
_____
_____
_____

4. Drama queens beware. As we discussed in Chapter 3, feeling and expressing your emotions is absolutely necessary for you to be healthy, complete and living your life to the fullest. If it is a matter of wanting to let off steam and be heard, use all the drama at your disposal. Again,

it's probably a good idea to let the person you are talking to know ahead of time if this is your intention. However, if you are talking with someone to get a specific point across, **how** you express your emotions determines how healthy you are. Are you speaking in a calm and empowered voice? If you find yourself using drama and emotions to manipulate others into the behavior you want, STOP.

Being a Mature and Empowered Listener

Now let's look at what it takes to be an active, empowered and involved listener. For our purposes here, listening means you stop what you are doing and focus all your attention on what someone is saying to you. Playing a computer game, working a crossword puzzle or watching TV while someone is talking to you is not listening. Laying the phone down to do something else and checking back every so often to see if the other person is still talking is not listening. Paying attention and focusing are the keys to being an active and involved listener. Many times people believe they are listening and they are not. They may even want to be a great listener but they have something blocking them.

Blocks that prevent you from really listening include:

1. Listening just so the other person will have to listen to you.
2. Thinking about what you are going to say when the other person is finished.
3. Thinking to yourself, or even asking, "How much longer is this going to take?"
4. Listening only for the parts you want to hear or hope you will hear.
5. Taking one word, one thought or one phrase and *running with it*.

> ***Running with it means focusing on one word, phrase or thought and making it mean all sorts of things in your own mind. You actually "go deaf" to the rest of what is being said.***

Observe your listening skills during the next week. Write down your observations to these questions, "Do I focus and listen attentively when someone is talking with me?" "Are there things I do when I am trying to listen that distract me?" "If there are, what are they?"

_____
_____
_____
_____

A great question to ask yourself and answer is, "How do I listen when someone is telling me something I don't want to hear?"

_____
_____
_____
_____

On being interrupted … most people dislike being interrupted. While we are not going to go into the psychology about that here, it is important to know, believe it or not, sometimes people don't even realize they are interrupting. These are some steps you can take to deal with interruptions:

1. The first time you are interrupted stop and say, "You are interrupting me. Please let me finish what I am saying."
2. If you are interrupted again, stop talking until the other person has stopped talking. Do not address the interruption. Ask if it is okay for you to continue what you were saying. If they say, "no," excuse yourself from the conversation and tell them you are willing to continue the conversation when they are ready to listen without interruption.
3. The third time you are interrupted, stop the conversation and tell them you are willing to continue the conversation when they are ready to listen without interruption. Give you and the other person a minimum of one hour before continuing the conversation. Make sure you get back to the conversation within the next 24 hours.

Take a few moments now to look and see when and under what circumstances you are most likely to interrupt someone else. Do you do this with some people more than others? If yes, with who?

_____
_____
_____
_____

Specific Guidelines for Clean and Clear Communication

1. Both people must want to communicate.

2. Stay focused on the present.

3. Pay attention to your feelings.

4. Be willing to understand one another.

5. Focus on finding a solution.

6. Try to see the other person's point of view. If you don't "get it," ask more questions until you do. In conflict, most of us primarily want to feel heard and understood.

7. Respond to criticism with empathy and understanding. Ask yourself what is true in what they are saying? For example, "I understand you feel angry." That doesn't mean you understand why they are angry. It means you get they are angry. It also means you don't get to give them your opinion about whether or not they should be angry or if it is okay for them to be angry. You get they are angry. That's all. If you need to respond with an explanation do it after you have heard them AND when they are able to hear you.

8. Own what is your stuff. Admit when you are wrong.

9. Use "I" messages. The other person is less likely to be defensive and

better able to hear you. Some people may still feel attacked. If they do feel attacked, there is not much you can do about it and still be in a healthy place.

Examples: Change, "You make me angry," to "I feel angry when you call me a witch." Change, "You are a jerk," to "I feel disrespected."

10. Look for compromise. Make it a win-win situation whenever possible.

11. Take a time out. It is perfectly okay to take a break and cool off. And sometimes it is even advisable. Just make sure you get back to the conversation. Never use the time out as a cop-out.

12. Be persistent. If you take a break, always come back to the conversation. Unless it is time to give up on the relationship, keep trying to communicate.

13. Ask for help if you need it. If you are having difficulty being respectful and the situation isn't improving, it is time to ask for professional help.

Non-verbal Communication

Communicating what is on your mind without speaking words is non-verbal communication. This includes facial expressions (winking, rolling your eyes, etc.) and body language (crossed arms or legs, leaning towards someone, leaning away from someone, etc.) The impression you give to others with your appearance (dress, hair, body odor, etc.) is also a form of non-verbal communication.

Warning! Keep in mind determining what you *think* a person is trying to communicate using only non-verbal clues is a huge mistake. All these things can give us clues as to what the person is trying to communicate but no one gesture alone or article of clothing can tell us everything.

Mixed Messages

Be aware of sending and receiving mixed messages. Being complimented with a sarcastic "Great job" puts clean and clear communication on high alert. Sarcasm is NOT clean and clear communication!

Three Steps for Clean and Clear Communication:

1. Begin your first sentence with, "When you…" Now describe the behavior of the other person you need to talk about. Be very specific. Using a label leaves room for misunderstandings and arguments. Example: Instead of saying, "When you call me names," say the name the person has called you. Such as, "When you call me a witch…."

2. Finish the first sentence with, "I feel…" Now describe how you feel when the person calls you a witch. Again, avoid labels. Be specific.

   Example: Instead of saying, "I feel upset," say, "When you call me a witch I feel hurt and angry," or however it is you feel. Be aware of the "on too long" syndrome and the drama temptation we talked about earlier. Eliminate both.

3. The second sentence would begin, "I want…" or, "Would you…" Then, you would describe the behavior you want.

   For example: "I want you to stop calling me a witch," or, "Please stop calling me a witch."

Keep in mind just because you have made a statement or request doesn't mean the other person is going to agree to or honor your request. It is at this point you will need to set some boundaries. There will be much more about setting and honoring boundaries in the next chapter. Remember, some people don't want to hear you just as there are some people you may not want to hear. These steps are not going to *make* either one of you want to hear the other person.

This is a very important exercise. Being honest in this exercise and taking the steps to complete this exercise will take you a long way in figuring yourself out and reclaiming pieces of yourself you have lost.

Make a list of the people you have been avoiding having a clean and clear conversation with. Make sure to include the topic you need to talk with them about.

_____
_____
_____
_____
_____

Practice using the three steps to clean and clear communication **before** actually talking to the person. All you need to start is the first three sentences. So, for each conversation you want to have fill in the blanks:

When you _____

I feel _____

I want _____

When you _____

I feel _____

I want _____

When you _____

I feel _____

I want _____

When you _____

I feel _____

I want _____

"The single biggest problem with communication is the illusion that is has taken place."
~George Bernard Shaw~

CHAPTER 9

Setting and Honoring Boundaries

Boundaries define limits. They draw a line in the sand that says, "Step across this line and *BAM!*" It may be a big *BAM* or a little *bam* depending on the boundary and how many times it has been crossed. Boundaries serve many purposes.

Boundaries:
- show what you think of yourself.
- teach others how to treat you.
- show up when you value yourself.
- are a result of you learning to listen to yourself.
- are about honoring what you want, what you don't want, what you need, what you don't need, what you like, what you don't like and what you want and don't want for yourself.
- come about when you believe you deserve the best life has to offer.

The bottom line, boundaries come from your self-worth and how you value yourself. Setting and honoring healthy boundaries indicate the level of your self-worth. When you honor your boundaries you are telling yourself and others how valuable you are.

What are **healthy** intentions for setting boundaries?

1. To protect your space.
2. To protect and take care of yourself no matter what happens, no matter where you go, no matter who is with you.

3. To be responsible for yourself in having a healthy relationship.
4. To honor yourself in your right to say, "No," to those things that aren't right for you or you don't want.
5. To respect yourself and your choices.

Setting boundaries out of anger, to get even or to teach the other person a lesson isn't going to work. Any of those motives would be making it all about them. Setting boundaries needs to be all about you!

Sometimes we set different boundaries for different people. No! Remember, boundaries are about you and that means the same boundary would apply to EVERYONE. Why, for example, would you accept poor behavior from a family member or a friend you wouldn't accept from a stranger? The answer is you wouldn't!

Setting boundaries has to start with awareness. In other words, you have to *get* that something isn't working. Setting boundaries just for the heck of it rarely happens. You can use the *Reclaiming Your Life Process* in Chapter 5. Using the same step by step awareness process in setting boundaries, Step 1 is **Awareness**, getting the insight that, "Oh, something is not quite right here."

Hint: If you are feeling anger, rage or irritation about a certain person or certain circumstances, you probably need to set a boundary. If you feel threatened around a particular situation or around a particular person, you probably need to set a boundary. If you find yourself whining or complaining about a situation or person, you probably need to set a boundary. If you feel sad, frustrated, suffocated or like a victim in a situation, you probably need to set a boundary. All this tells you, "Oh, something is not quite right here."

Step 2, **Awareness of the Truth**, is a realization something like, "Oh, I'm being used. I always say yes to this person even when I want to say no. I have no boundaries."

Step 3, ***Experiencing the Truth***, is to experience not having boundaries. How does it feel to realize you are being used? How does it feel when you always say yes to another person even when you want to say no? How does it feel to not think enough of yourself to say no when you want or need to? How does it feel to not have a boundary? Make sure you are actually *feeling* and *experiencing* not having that boundary.

Step 4, ***Accept the Truth***, is to accept you don't have boundaries. And, to accept you don't have boundaries in a situation without beating yourself up about it. In other words, accept you don't have boundaries in this situation without judgment. If you are beating yourself up by telling yourself what a pathetic human being you are for having put up with this for so long, you have judgment and you are not really accepting. You are too busy focusing on your judgment.

In Step 5, Reclaiming Your Power, you set and honor your boundary.

Three Steps to Setting Boundaries

Before taking these three steps, make sure you have had a clean and clear conversation with the person before setting a boundary. This concept was explained in the previous chapter. Sometimes, although rarely, the conversation is enough to clear up the situation and you don't need to use these steps.

Remember to have a "changing of the rules talk" as an introduction to the three steps. You may say something like, "I know I have allowed you to call me a witch in the past. I am now changing the rule and I will no longer allow myself to be called a witch. Here is my new rule about calling me a witch."

1. Begin your first sentence with, "If you..." Now describe the behavior

of the other person you find unacceptable. Be very specific. Using a label leaves room for misunderstandings and arguments.

Example: Instead of saying, "If you call me names," you would say the name the person has called you. Such as, "If you call me a witch…"

2. Finish this sentence with, "I will…" Now describe what you will do when that person calls you a witch. Again, avoid labels. Be specific.

Example: Instead of saying, "When you call me a witch I will be upset," you would say, "When you call me a witch I will hang up the phone," or whatever it is you will do if they call you a witch. Be careful of the drama temptations in this step.

3. The second sentence would begin, "If you continue to call me a witch I will…" Then you would describe the action you will take.

Example: "If you continue to call me a witch I will end the friendship," or whatever it is you will do if they continue to call you a witch. It is not always necessary or appropriate to share this third step with the other person immediately. If your third step is, "I will end the friendship," you might want to give them the opportunity to stop calling you a witch without going to more drastic measures. Sometimes this third step can seem like a threat if shared too soon and can set up resistance on the part of the other person. It is necessary for you to know within yourself what the third step is even if you don't share it immediately.

Be prepared to follow through on honoring your boundaries. ***You will be tested!*** It is not enough to set boundaries. The next step is to be willing to do whatever it takes for YOU to honor and enforce your boundaries. If you are not willing to do this, don't even bother setting the boundary. You become a victim when you expect others to honor your boundary just because you set it. When **you** honor your boundary no one else has a choice. Another key to honoring your boundary is to have no attachment to the choice they make. That way you can follow through on **you** honoring your boundary. Having no attachment to the outcome means you follow through no matter what and that may include feeling whatever feelings come up and honoring your boundary anyway.

Example: "If you do not put your clothes in the hamper I will not launder them." In this example you must be prepared to have a pile, or piles, of dirty clothes, on the floor for as long as it takes the other person to run out of clothes. You must also be willing to have the person wear dirty clothes until *they* get tired of wearing dirty clothes. As soon as you pick up even one article of clothing you have dishonored your boundary. Never set a consequence you are not prepared to enforce.

Then there is the concept of **Wiggle Room.** Wiggle room is giving the other person the opportunity to learn and remember the new boundary. It is perfectly okay to remind someone of the new boundary and remind them of the changing of the rules talk. Once. Maybe twice. Maybe three times. Be careful though. Too much wiggle room can put you right back where you started. Too much wiggle room and your boundary no longer exists. Even during the wiggle room phase, you do not tolerate being treated poorly.

Setting Boundaries vs. Manipulation

When determining whether you are setting a boundary or being manipulative, ask yourself, "What is my intention for setting this boundary?" You may want to review the list of healthy reasons for setting boundaries found at the beginning of this chapter. If you are attached to the outcome it is probably manipulation. If you can honestly say you really don't care whether they honor the boundary or take the consequences, it is probably a boundary. It is almost certainly manipulation if you are trying to control the outcome or someone else's behavior. It is probably manipulation if you are not willing or prepared to experience loss (friendship, political/public position, job, status, etc.).

Questions to Ask Yourself When Setting Boundaries

1. Do I just want to be right?
2. Do I want them to change?
3. Am I attempting to manipulate another person's behavior?
4. Am I attached to the outcome?
5. What am I willing to lose in order to honor my boundary?

Take some time now and make a list of all the areas where you need to set boundaries. Also, write down how you feel when you are in those situations.

_____

_____

_____

_____

The idea in the above exercise is to increase your awareness. You need to recognize where you don't have boundaries before you can set boundaries.

Having awareness of how you experience not having a boundary is a great motivation to begin to set and honor your boundaries.

For practice, select one of the areas from above you want to practice setting a boundary around. Pick the area you think is the easier one to start with and answer these questions.

Why am I setting this boundary?

_____
_____
_____
_____
_____

What is my intention for setting this boundary?

_____
_____
_____
_____
_____

What is my changing of the rules statement?

_____
_____
_____
_____

_____

_____

Now follow the 3 steps to setting and honoring a boundary:

Step 1:	If you	
Step 2:	I will	
Step 3:	If you continue to	
	I will	

The final step is to set your boundary and honor it.

It will serve you to pay attention to what feelings, experiences and thoughts come up for you as you are practicing setting and honoring your boundaries. Paying attention will show you the issues you may need to deal with in order to continue your journey.

Now go back to your list of areas where you need to set boundaries and select another area and repeat this process. Continue to repeat this process until you have set boundaries in all the areas you listed. By using this process you may discover additional boundaries you need to set. Remember to stay aware of the signals which tell you it is time to set a boundary. Those signals are on the second page of this chapter. As a reminder and review for yourself, write those signals here:

_____

_____

_____

_____

_____

Remember:

1. You cannot set boundaries with someone else and at the same time take care of their feelings. That doesn't mean you have to be a raving witch or a flaming behind. It does mean you have to hold the other people in your life accountable for their own feelings and choices.
2. When you first begin to set boundaries you will have all sorts of doubts and you may experience feelings that are new to you. Sometimes setting boundaries may feel just plain wrong. This feeling is what I call a withdrawal symptom. It does get better as you practice setting and honoring your boundaries.
3. Be prepared to follow through and enforce your boundary.
4. You will be tested! This is almost a 100% guarantee.
5. Set your boundary clearly, in as few words as possible.

Now it is time for the butt on the piano bench ….. practice, practice, practice.

Goal Setting Again?!

I know it's tempting to skip goal setting 'cause you've heard it so many times before
BUT
please read it anyway.
There is one additional step that will serve you!

CHAPTER 10

Goals, Affirmations and Achieving

The groans, the eye rolls and the big sighs are always in abundance when this topic comes up. "Not goals and affirmations AGAIN!" "I've done goals and affirmations a million times. They don't work." "I hate goals and affirmations."

The truth is you have to work goals and affirmations. They are an inanimate object, just a tool, but a very useful tool. Goals and affirmations do not guarantee anything. Keep something else in mind. You don't have to write goals for everything, only for that which is important to you or for that which you find hard to achieve.

Sometimes people are unclear about the difference between a goal and an affirmation. Many times people want to call their affirmations goals. Goals and affirmations may sound very much alike when you say them out loud, but there is a definite distinction between the two. It is important to understand this difference in order to use them effectively.

The Difference between Goals and Affirmations

Think of a goal as the destination or the end result. Working towards having the money to buy a hardtop convertible is a goal. Dieting and exercising to fit into size 6 jeans is a goal. Wanting a three bedroom home on an acre of land in southern Minnesota, wanting a 60 inch plasma flat screen TV, wanting a larger salary or more clients are all examples of a goal.

Think of an affirmation as a statement declaring something is true.

Saying out loud, "I have a hardtop convertible," is an affirmation. "I fit into size 6 jeans," is an affirmation.

Why Use Goals?

Hint: Remember how the subconscious mind works. Review Chapter 3, if necessary.

Use goals because they reinforce, both in your conscious and your subconscious mind, exactly what it is you say you want. The use of goals keeps the awareness of what you want at the front of the line in your mind. When you set your goal clearly and exactly, your subconscious mind begins to work with you towards the achievement of your goal. When you build the picture of what you want, your subconscious mind begins to build a file for your goal. Each affirmation you use for your goal goes into the file. Each picture you create for your goal goes into the file. Remember, the subconscious mind is literal, so whatever you put in the goal file your mind sees as true and already accomplished.

How Do Goals Really Work?

Hint: Remember how the subconscious mind works.

Repetition, repetition, repetition, repetition, repetition, repetition… You get the idea. Because the subconscious mind hears and stores everything and responds to what is stored, you want to make sure you have as much stored in your mind as you can about what you want. You want the goal file to be huge and overshadow the files with the "I can't do its" in them.

Another **Hint:** Remember the primary learning modes.

In Chapter 3 you had the opportunity to discover your primary learning mode. With this way of setting goals and writing affirmations, you are able to set it up so you are using your primary learning mode and reinforcing your other modes of learning at the same time. So, if your primary learning mode is auditory, you may want to recite your goals and affirmations out loud or record them and listen to them daily. If your primary learning mode is kinesthetic, it may serve you best to write your goals and affirmations daily. If your primary learning mode is visual, writing and reading your goals daily may be the best way for you to reinforce them. Of course, using all three modes every day is the best. Because you are focusing on using your primary learning mode, it is much easier for your mind to accept and integrate your goal.

Six Steps to Setting Powerful Goals:

1. **Write a powerful goal statement.** You do this by first choosing your goal and being as specific and clear and detailed as you possibly can. Actually, what you are doing in this step is painting a picture in your mind of what your goal looks like, feels like, sounds like and maybe even smells like.

    One way to have a powerful goal statement is to write down *exactly* what you want. If your goal is to lose weight, you would say, "I weigh _____ pounds." If your goal is to lower your blood pressure, you would say, "My blood pressure is 120/80." If you want more income you would say, "My income is _____." To repeat: Write down or say *exactly* what you want. In other words, make sure your goal is *definite* and *specific*.

    Another example: "I am going to give a talk at school (work, church, etc.) and I won't be nervous." What is the word in that sentence that immediately stands out and will probably be flashing through your mind? Nervous? Yes, nervous. Instead of saying what you won't be, say what you will be. "I am going to give a talk at school and I am calm and relaxed." To repeat again: Write down or say *exactly* what you want.

When you are setting a goal for something like a car, carry this first step even farther. Go online or go to the dealership and get a picture of the car you want, in exactly the color and style you want. Put the picture on your bathroom mirror, near your computer or in your wallet. In fact, put the picture in all three places. Every time you see the picture it reinforces the goal of the car in your mind.

Take the time right now to practice these steps. Pick a goal for yourself. Describe your goal to the smallest detail. Include everything. What will it look like? What will it sound like? What will it smell like? What will it feel like?

_____
_____
_____
_____

When you have finished describing your goal take another few minutes and add at least three more details about your goal.

_____
_____
_____
_____

2. **Make sure your goal is realistic.** Having a goal of 150 new clients for your business this week is probably a bit unrealistic, depending on your business, of course. Having a goal of five new clients this week is much more realistic and attainable. Having a goal of losing 20 pounds in the next week is probably unrealistic. Determine what would be realistic. Losing two or three pounds in the next week is realistic.

3. **Set a specific date by which you will have accomplished your goal.** Make sure to include the month, the day AND the year. Remember, the subconscious mind is literal so including the year is critical. What is the exact date you want to have achieved the goal you wrote down above? _____

   When writing the date, use the phrase "on or before" followed by the date. Because your subconscious mind is literal using this phrase gives your mind room to accept your goal earlier than what you stated.

4. **Write your goal statement.** Put all the information you have about your goal into one simple, complete sentence.

   Example: "On or before Jan. 15, 2020, I have a hardtop convertible."

   Using the goal you described above and the date you want to achieve your goal write your powerful goal statement below.

   _____
   _____
   _____
   _____

Because you have done all the preparation in step one and two the goal statement will automatically bring up the "picture" of your goal in your mind.

Make sure you write the phrase "on or before" before the date you have chosen. Also, if your goal involves having a specific amount of money make sure you add the phrase "or more" to your statement.

Example: "On or before Oct. 1, 2020 I have $10,000 or more in my savings account."

Again, because your subconscious mind is literal, adding "or more" leaves room for you to have more than the amount you want.

5. **Figure the cost of your goal.** You *have* to know the cost of your goal. How can you possibly make an informed decision about whether or not you want a particular goal if you don't have ALL of the information? You can't. Include everything, right down to the penny. The cost of your goal is the money it is going to cost you to achieve your goal. Dig deep to find the cost of your goal. Many times it seems as if there is no cost. Beware. This can be a place that can become a block if you have not really researched well. This is also the step in the process people seem to dislike the most. They don't want to have to figure it all out. Close enough is not good enough unless close enough to your goal is good enough for you.

For example, if you have a goal of eating healthier, healthy food is sometimes more expensive. Figure the difference in the cost of your food. If you have a goal of exercising more, even if you don't join a gym or get a coach, what about the cost of those new running shoes? What about the cost of shoe laces? What about the cost of a bigger water bottle? What about the extra gas money to drive to the gym twice a day? Make sure you figure it all out so you don't get any surprises down the road. Again, it's a matter of getting all the information.

In addition, be careful about minimizing any part of the cost. "It's only a little bit of postage." "I just have to have a few copies made." These costs add up so make sure you are as aware as possible about all the costs of your goal.

Again, look for the cost, even if it doesn't appear as if there are any. Keep track of the cost of your goal down to the penny. Even if you are using something you already have, you had to pay for it at some point in time and the cost should be added to the cost of your current goal. Only with complete and accurate information can you make an informed decision as to whether or not you want to pay that much for your goal. Yes, this process is tedious and it's in your best interest. So, do it anyway.

You selected a goal earlier in this chapter. You wrote a goal statement with the exact date, including the year, for the achievement of your goal. Now, figure the exact cost in dollars and cents, right down to the penny for your goal. Challenge yourself to find all the hidden costs.

Cost	Item or Service	Cost	Item or Service

Here is the additional step I promised would serve you and make a big difference in whether or not you accomplish your goal.

6. **Figure out the price of your goal.** The price of your goal has absolutely nothing to do with money. The price of your goal has absolutely nothing to do with money. The price of your goal has absolutely nothing to do with money. This is not a typo. The price of your goal has absolutely nothing to do with money. Anything to do with money involved with your goal will go in the cost section of setting your goal. Determining the price of your goal is a step many people don't even know about. There are those people that know about it and don't want to do it. This step requires you to be willing to see things about yourself you may not be pleased about. This step also requires you to be honest with yourself. You must be willing to see your shortcomings and blocks and be willing to work through them. In fact, willingness to see and accept your shortcomings and blocks is a price you will have to pay for your goal.

This step is probably the one that takes the most time and deliberation. It is also the step most likely to bring up feelings and experiences you would just as soon avoid. But, here we go again, how can you possibly make an informed decision about whether or not you want a particular goal if you don't have all the information? Yes, it is tedious, boring and probably uncomfortable, but do it anyway.

The price of your goal may include giving up time with your family, giving up your weekly golf game or giving up choir rehearsal on Monday night. It may mean giving up some income or time away from your job. Remember, learning something new is a price because it may take time away from something else or it may mean you have to deal with feelings that come up while you are trying to learn something new. When you realize what you might have to give up or what you are going to have to do to learn, you may decide you really don't want your goal that much after all.

The price of your goal may mean overcoming an emotional issue that has been blocking you from your goal. It may be something as seemingly simple as overcoming fear of riding in elevators in order to take the great new job on the tenth floor. This may even mean an increase in cost. Or, it may mean the price you have to pay is the hard work and possible turmoil you go through to overcome the emotional block. One of the prices you might have to pay is to overcome your resistance, resistance to this process, maybe even resistance to your goal.

Sometimes the price you have to pay may turn into a goal all its own. For example, if your goal is to climb Mt. Everest and you weigh 400 pounds, one of the prices you will have to pay to achieve that goal is to lose weight. In this case, it is best to have losing weight a goal in and of itself. If losing weight is your goal, a price you will have to pay is to exercise more. Then exercise turns into a separate goal. Having it as a separate goal will help you give the goal the focus you need to accomplish it.

The price of a goal is specific and unique to each individual person. Stop comparing yourself to any other person. Each of you will be paying a different price for what seems to be the same goal.

You selected a goal earlier in this chapter. You wrote a goal statement with the exact date, including the year, for the achievement of your goal. You have figured the exact cost for your goal in dollars and cents, right down to the penny. Now take the time to determine the prices you are probably going to have to pay in order to achieve your goal. Remember, the price of your goal is specific and unique to you.

_____

_____

_____

It is at this point, based on the cost and the price, you decide whether or not you still want the goal. Ask yourself if you can, and if you are willing, to invest the dollars needed to achieve your goal. If you don't have the finances currently, what are you willing to do to get the finances?

It is also at this point you ask yourself if you are willing to absorb additional costs for your goal should they come up.

Next, ask yourself if you are willing to pay the price you will have to pay in order to achieve your goal. Also, ask yourself if you are willing to pay any additional prices that may come up.

If all your answers to these questions are a genuine, honest, "yes," go forward with putting into place what is needed to achieve your goal.

Based on what you now know about the cost and the price of your goal, do you still want the goal you chose earlier in this chapter?

_____

If you decide you no longer want the goal based on what you have discovered about the cost and the price, ask yourself if there is a way you can modify the goal, the cost or the price to make it more acceptable to you. If yes, what would the modification be?

_____
_____
_____
_____

If there isn't a healthy way to do the modification, drop the goal and move on to something else. As part of your decision you get the opportunity to work through all your judgments, opinions, beliefs, expectations and rules about dropping a goal.

Again, there are times when this whole process feels tedious. It can get boring and frustrating. These are the very reasons some people want to avoid the whole process. At times, it doesn't seem as though you know the answers and you ask yourself why you are going through all this cost and price process. After all, all you wanted was the car, the house, to lose the weight or to become more confident!

You go through this process because determining the cost and the price gives you clarity about what you say you want. Only with all this information can you truthfully and clearly answer the question about whether or not you want the goal. Having all this information gives you a much better chance of achieving your goal because you know what you are facing towards achieving your goal.

Now that you are certain you want the goal you have described, it is time to start taking the steps toward attaining your goal. One very important step is to begin to use affirmations to support yourself in achieving your goal. The affirmations you use will be based on the work you have already done in determining your goal. First, a little more information about affirmations.

Affirmations and How They Work

Remember from the beginning of this chapter that an affirmation is a statement declaring something is true. There are some people who think just because they recite an affirmation everything is going to change and they are going to get what they want. Please remember there is nothing magical about affirmations. Using them doesn't automatically sprinkle "grant-three-wishes dust" over you and your problems are solved. However, affirmations are very useful tools and are a natural follow up and support in helping you achieve your goals.

How do affirmations work? An affirmation is a tool to help you stay focused on your goal. An affirmation is also a tool to use to program, or re-program, your subconscious mind to help you achieve your goal. Affirmations are a very powerful way to reinforce, in your subconscious mind, what you say you want in life.

Remember the files in your subconscious mind? Using affirmations is a way of making the file that says what you are, or have, bigger than the files that say what you aren't, or don't have. For example, if you have a file that says you are stupid, you want to build a bigger file saying you are smart. You will need to use every opportunity you can to reinforce how smart you are. No, saying five million times, "I am smart," does not make you smart. But, then someone else telling you five million times you are stupid didn't make you stupid either. At some level you believed it. Remember, this is a way of re-training your subconscious mind.

Affirmations may also work to bring up issues you were unaware are a problem. For example, you may think you are finally open to having a healthy and loving relationship in your life so you begin to use the affirmation, "I am open and willing to enjoy a loving and healthy relationship." You may find yourself becoming anxious or even sad and angry about the affirmation. You may be resistant, or even flatly refuse to use the affirmation, let alone, take steps towards developing relationships. This is a good indication you may have some other work to do before being able to use this particular affirmation comfortably and effectively.

Tips and Guidelines for Wording Your Affirmations

1. Make sure the affirmation is in the present tense. For example, change, "I will be calm and relaxed during my speech," to, "I am calm and relaxed during my speech."

2. Make sure you tell yourself what it is you want. For example, change, "I won't eat sweets and fats," to, "I eat fresh fruits, fresh vegetables and lean protein." Another example might be changing, "I won't be nervous," to, "I am calm and relaxed."
3. Make sure the affirmation is definite. (Calm and relaxed.)
4. Make sure the affirmation is specific. For example, instead of saying, "I eat good things for me," say, "I eat fruits and vegetables."
5. Make sure your affirmation is realistic. Instead of saying, "I lose 25 pounds this week," say, "I lose 3 pounds this week."

At first some of these changes will seem awkward. This is because it is a new way of communicating with yourself. The awkwardness will pass as you practice and gain more experience in saying things in a way your subconscious mind will hear and incorporate them better.

You will notice the tips and guidelines for writing your affirmations are the same as the steps for writing your goal statement. With affirmations you will use a shortened version of your goal statement that will serve as a reminder to your subconscious mind of the entire goal. It will serve you to use affirmations that are related to your goal statement, but not necessarily part of it.

Using the tips and guidelines above, write two affirmations to use with the goal you chose earlier in this chapter. For example, if your goal was to lose weight, one of your affirmations might be, "I am slim, trim and healthy." Write your specific affirmations on the lines below.

_____
_____
_____
_____

When Affirmations Aren't "Working"

The first thing to consider when you think your affirmations are not working is to understand what you mean by not working. They may be working just fine. If by not working, you mean you are feeling anxious and upset by them, this is a good indication you may have some other work to do before you are able to use this particular affirmation comfortably. This is one of those times when part of your journey involves learning to become comfortable feeling uncomfortable.

If by not working, you mean you haven't seen the results you want, you need to first consider how long you have been using the affirmation. Affirmations do not create direct, immediate results. Remember, using affirmations is a way of making the file in your subconscious mind saying what you are, or what you have, bigger than the files saying what you aren't, or don't have. Building the new files will take time. You ask, "How long?" As long as it takes is the answer. Not a very satisfying answer but bottom line is it takes as long as it takes. There is no magical number. Also, make sure you are taking the other necessary steps toward your goal and not relying on the "grant-three-wishes dust."

When it seems like the affirmations are not working, here are two other things to double check. First of all, go back and make sure you have followed the tips and guidelines exactly as they are written.

Next, make sure you are using only two or three affirmations at a time. More than that can get confusing. Keep the affirmations as simple as possible. Descriptions are unnecessary in affirmations. Affirmations are snapshot statements reminding you of your goal.

On the next page, you will find a worksheet that brings these steps together in one place. It also includes gentle reminders along the way to help you stay on track in the goal setting process. Remember to complete each step on the worksheet in order to achieve the best results.

Goals and Affirmations Worksheet

Goal Description: (Be specific and detailed. Add the phrase "or more" if your goal is money-related.)

_____

_____

_____

_____

Goal Completion Date: _____
(Make sure to use the phrase "on or before.")

Goal Statement:

_____

_____

_____

_____

Cost: (How much money will it cost you, down to the penny?)

_____

_____

_____

_____

Price: (Has nothing to do with money!)

_____
_____
_____
_____

Based on what I know about the cost and price, do I still want this goal? _____

If no, is there a way I can modify the goal, cost or price to make it more acceptable? _____

If yes, what would that modification be?

_____
_____
_____
_____

Yes, I do still want this goal:

Do I need to break this goal into smaller goals? _____ If the answer is yes, start another goal sheet for the smaller goals and complete the process for each smaller goal.

Affirmations to use:

_____
_____
_____
_____

Final Test:

Double check your goal and your affirmation statements with these questions:
- Am I saying what I want?
- Is it definite?
- Is it specific?
- Is it in the present tense?
- Is it realistic?

The Beginning

Bibliography

Bryan, W.J., Jr. (1961b). The Walking Zombie Syndrome. *Journal of the American Institute of Hypnosis,* 2 (3), 10-18.

Bryan, W.J., Jr. (1964). Ponce de Leon Syndrome. *Journal of the American Institute of Hypnosis,* 6 (4), 31-42.

Hull, William F., Prenatal Oxygen Deprivation, the Source of Birth Trauma. *Medical Hypnoanalysis,* 1984, 7-16.

Koelling, Lloyd H., Birth Trauma and Psychosomatic Illness in Children and Adolescents. *Medical Hypnoanalysis,* 1984, 34-41.

Kubler-Ross, Elisabeth, (1969). *On Death and Dying.* New York: Scribner.

Scott, John A., Sr. (1983*). Hypnoanalysis for Individual and Marital Psychotherapy.* New York: Gardner Press, Inc.

Scott, John A., Sr., Scott, John A., Jr. Age Regressions to Birth. *Medical Hypnoanalysis,* 1984, 17-33.

Verny, M.D., Kelly, John. (1981). *The Secret Life of the Unborn Child.* New York: Dell Publishing.

Appendix

Duly Noted!!!

Symptoms Worksheet

So, how do you know if you have "checked out" or lost pieces of yourself? Mostly, your life will be out of balance. You will experience extremes of normal everyday "stuff" like sleeping too much or not being able to sleep at all. You may notice a big decrease in your appetite or a big increase in your appetite. You may experience no interest in sex or an extremely high interest in sex. Remember, the key here is *extremes*. Take some time now and complete the awareness worksheet below.

Please circle yes or no to each of the questions below. More often than not do you…

Say "yes" when you want to say "no?"	Yes	No
Say "I don't need any help," when you do?	Yes	No
Say "That doesn't bother me," but it does?	Yes	No
Say "Just one more drink won't hurt."	Yes	No
Say "I am not mad," when you really are?	Yes	No
Say "I can quit smoking any time I want."	Yes	No
Say "I am fine. Everything is okay," when it isn't?	Yes	No
Say "I can drop this weight any time I want," but you don't?	Yes	No

Smile when you really want to snap?	Yes	No
Bite your tongue when you have something to say.	Yes	No

Are you experiencing any of these on a regular basis?		
Feeling unreasonably tired	Yes	No
Loss of confidence	Yes	No
Procrastination	Yes	No
Inability to sleep	Yes	No
Sleeping too much	Yes	No
Eating binges	Yes	No
Feeling like a total failure	Yes	No
Lack of excitement for life	Yes	No
Spending binges	Yes	No
Guilt	Yes	No
Anxiety	Yes	No
Lack of joy	Yes	No

Life Awareness Worksheet

Name _____

Birthday _____

Birth Place _____

Time of birth _____

1. What's the problem (your primary concerns or issues)? Please use complete sentences.

   _____

   _____

   _____

   _____

2. How long has this been a problem for you?

   _____

   _____

   _____

   _____

3. Present Occupation: _____

   Like/dislike your job? _____

   If you could do anything you wanted as an occupation, what would it be?

   _____
   _____
   _____
   _____

4. Life Scale

On a scale of 0-10 (10 being the absolute best, 0 being the absolute worst)	
Looking at everything that is going on in your life, what number are you right now?	
What is the lowest number you have ever been in your whole life?	
What is the highest number you have ever been in your whole life?	

5. When you were born or when your mother was carrying you, was there any kind of a problem?

_____
_____
_____
_____
_____

6. List all childhood diseases and, if possible, the age at which you had the disease.

_____
_____
_____
_____
_____

7. List any hospitalizations or surgeries and the age you were when they occurred.

_____
_____
_____
_____

8. List any current medical conditions.

   _____
   _____
   _____
   _____

9. List any traumatic events in your life and the age at which they occurred. What is important to keep in mind here is whether it was traumatic for YOU.

   _____
   _____
   _____
   _____

10. Make a list of things in your life you feel guilty about and your age at the time the guilt started.

    _____
    _____
    _____
    _____

11. List what you consider to be your successes.

   _____
   _____
   _____
   _____
   _____

12. Is there anything in your life you don't want anyone to find out about?

   _____
   _____
   _____
   _____
   _____

13. Write down anything else you think might be helpful to you in achieving more awareness in your life. For example: income level, educational level, relationships, etc.

   _____
   _____
   _____
   _____
   _____

Words and Phrases Exercise

Listed below are a number of various words, thoughts and phrases. Please respond quickly with the very first word, thought, phrase, emotion or idea that pops into your mind.

1. Sweet	
2. Fear	
3. Anger	
4. If only	
5. There must be	
6. I know I'm stressed when I	
7. I always	
8. All my life	
9. I felt like dying when	
10. Red	
11. I'm just like	
12. Please	
13. It all started when	

14. Kindness	
15. Death	
16. I don't want to disappoint	
17. I'm just tired of	
18. It got worse when	
19. I never	
20. Success	
21. Exercises like this	
22. Begin a sentence with the word, "who"	
23. Career	
24. Confidence	
25. Relax	

Tree Exercise

In the space provided below, draw a tree.

1. Draw a line across the top of the tree, like the top of the tree has hit the ceiling.
2. Draw a line at the base of the tree (where it meets the ground).
3. Draw another line midway between the top line and the bottom line.
4. Draw another line halfway between the middle line and the top line.

5. Draw another line halfway between the middle line and the bottom line. Your tree should now be divided into 4 equal parts.
6. Write your present age on the top line.
7. Put a zero on the bottom line.
8. Divide your present age by 2. Put that number on the middle line.
9. Divide the number on the middle line by 2. Put that number on the line between the middle line and the bottom line.
10. Take the number that is on the line between the middle and the bottom line and add it to the number on the middle line. Put this new number on the line between the middle line and the top line.

Ready For More Figuring Yourself Out

- Live Workshops
- Retreats
- Teleclasses
- Books
- eBooks
- MP3 Downloads
- Private Coaching

Visit FiguringYourselfOut.com where you can learn about and sign up for upcoming workshops, retreats, teleclasses or other events; as well as download additional resources, eBooks and MP3's.

Contact Pat Honiotes
Pat@FiguringYourselfOut.com
Phone: (602) 541-5508

www.ingramcontent.com/pod-product-compliance
Lightning Source LLC
Chambersburg PA
CBHW080246170426
43192CB00014BA/2586